MIKE SIMMONS

OUR GREATEST OPPORTUNITY

Is the Great Commission For Today?

CHRISTIANOLOGY SERIES

ALL SCRIPTURE IS THE KING JAMES VERSION OF THE BIBLE

Christianology
Publications

Copyright 2020 Christianology Publications

No part of this publication may be reproduced or copied in any form without written permission from the copyright owner.

ISBN 978-0-578-58130-9

TABLE OF CONTENTS

1. What in the World is Missing?
2. A Word to the Wise from the Heart
3. What are We Fighting For?
4. It's a Matter of Life or Death
5. Does Anybody Know the Time?
6. Here Comes the Judge
7. Go Ye Therefore
8. Many are Called, Few are Chosen
9. The Soul Patrol
10. The Lordship of Jesus Christ
11. Accepting Christ
12. Revival Comes by Salvation

Introduction

The culture of Christianity has changed from a reverent and sacred disposition to a casual approach to church and worship.

Many points of justification have been made defending this position of a carefree style to move away from hypocrisy and other forms of pretense.

In earlier times, the church would separate worldliness from entering the realm of spirituality, but at the present, it is invited to the extent to where the lines have become blurred and true conversion has become questionable.

Getting back to evangelism by the book will bring back the purpose for Almighty God sending Jesus Christ into the world to die and commission true transformation for every living soul.

It is the responsibility of the church today to keep this mandate alive to introduce salvation to every person regardless of the opposition from the enemy and society.

"Our Greatest Opportunity" to serve God has come as the "Great Commission" in partnership with the Holy Spirit to change our culture and bring revival back to the world.

"The chief danger that confronts the coming century will be religion without the Holy Ghost, Christianity without Christ, forgiveness without repentance, salvation without regeneration, politics without God, heaven without hell." (William Booth)

Chapter One

What in the World is Missing?

What shall we say then? Shall we continue in silence that bliss may abound? God forbid. "Bliss" is not real in the Christian life unless you are obeying the commands of God. The proper term in a spiritual form would be the fruit of "Joy," only produced by the Holy Spirit.

Am I saying that a Christian can't have full joy unless he or she is obeying God? Most experience some joy if they go to church, read their Bible, pray fervently, and obey the preacher. The Spirit-filled Christian lives the victorious joy all the time.

"The Church suffers today from a saddening lack of old-fashioned, simple-hearted, over flowing, Christian joy. We have plenty of knowledge, plenty of enthusiasm and denominational zeal, but Christians and churches that started out in revival fires are living in the smoke." 1(Vance Havner)

But, don't take too much thought about the "Great Commission" when you happen to read it, or perhaps the Pastor may mention it in a message; or you might unlock the undenying truth.

According to the Barna Research Group, the "Great Commission" cannot be accurately defined by 86% of adult Americans.1 Most Christians today have never heard, or if they have, they never understood what the implications are

---

1 Vance Havner, Nelson's Complete Book of Stories, Illustrations,& Quotes, 499

of a soul being lost for all of eternity. This subject is too personal for some. 2

Post- Modern World and the Great Commission

The ministers of today are cutting short the blessing, rewards, and opportunities to experience a full joy for the listener. But, you can't blame the Pastor, Preacher, or Christian teacher because, most likely, the opportunity to witness or lead someone to the Lord has never been a priority in the church where they started. The Church has become a community of well-intended individuals hoping and praying to connect with everyone inside and outside the Church. Thank God that someone is trying to show the path to an un- churched, ungodly community.

We really need to be careful that we don't replace good intentions in the place of the "Great Commission" given to us by the Lord Jesus Christ in Matthew 28: 18-20, *"And Jesus came and spake unto them, saying, All power is given unto me in heaven and in earth. Go ye therefore, and teach all nations, baptizing them in the name of the Father, and of the Son, and of the Holy Ghost: Teaching them to observe all things whatsoever I have commanded you: and, lo, I am with you alway, even unto the end of the world. Amen."*

Our greatest teacher did not forget to not only mention his intentions here, but, he gave us a command and commission with promise. I can't see where he was vague about the purpose of reaching the world here at all. Let's take these verses into focus for an investigation:

2 www.barna.org, Is Evangelism Going Out of Style?, Dec. 17, 2013

- ❖ Vs. 18 – He spoke unto his disciples about his omnipotence that cannot be matched; "all" power in heaven and earth. That covers it "all."
- ❖ Vs. 19 – What are we to do? Teach "all" nations; the gospel message is the evangelistic message of the entire Bible; the death, burial, and resurrection.
- ❖ Vs. 19 – Baptizing them; the identification of the gospel message. The "New Life" (Rom. 6:3-4), ordained by the Godhead; the Father, the Son, and the Holy Ghost.
- ❖ Vs. 20 – Teach them to observe "all" things whatsoever I have commanded you. John 14:26 tells us that we will be reminded by the Holy Ghost. "...and bring all things to your remembrance, whatsoever I have said unto you." The perpetual message with no mention of phasing it out.
- ❖ Vs. 20 – The promise of his presence with his almighty power. The message and the commission have been sealed; "Thus saith the Lord."

So why is the "Great Commission" our "Greatest Opportunity" of all ages? It is like asking why Salvation is so important. The answer is best stated this way; "God's eternal plan, with God's eternal power, with God's eternal purpose."

Does God have the means to fulfill all this? Can we join God for a new Spiritual Revival?

<u>The Plan</u> - Share the Eternal Promise

- o John 3:16, "For God so loved the world, that he gave his only begotten Son, that whosoever believeth in him should not perish, but have everlasting life."
- o I Peter 2:9, "But ye are a chosen generation, a royal priesthood, an holy nation, a peculiar people; that ye

should shew forth the praises of him who hath called you out of darkness into his marvelous light."

The Power -   Prove His Personal Presence
- Romans 1:16, "For I am not ashamed of the gospel of Christ: for it is the power of God unto salvation to everyone that believeth..."

The Purpose -   Share the Message

It is a wonderful thing to think that a loving God provided a Savior for us, and to save us from a sinful life and eternity in hell. What did we do to deserve this kind of mercy? And, God gives us the highest calling of carrying forward the glorious message of how Jesus came to this earth to die on a cross, shedding his blood to cleanse and to give us eternal life. Only Almighty God can do this!

Follow Me

Most people are convinced that they do not possess the ability, faculty, or quality to be a participant in our greatest opportunity, but deep down, they would like to see someone get saved. The courage to be trained is the first step, and once you have won someone to the Lord, you will never turn back. Note that the Bible does not list witnessing and soul-winning as Spiritual Gifts, because they are not Spiritual Gifts. (I Cor. 12, Eph. 4) God gives everyone the opportunity to make a difference in people's lives. It is what makes the opportunity wonderful and great. You will never have to wonder if you are in God's will, like some do, when you are partaking in the "Great Commission". In the gospel of Matthew 4:19, Jesus said to two of his brethren, *"Follow me, and I will make you fishers of men."* What do you think could be running through the minds of these two, namely, Peter and Andrew? In Matthew 4:20, *"And they straightway left their nets..."* Then James and John were next; verse 22, *"And they immediately left the ship and their father, and followed him."*

Some have recognized that no matter what, the greatest opportunity in their life, after they are saved, is to join God's purpose of gleaning this earth, shining the light, and rescuing a dying world that's hour has come. *"He that loveth his life shall lose it; and he that hateth his life in this world shall keep it unto life eternal. If any man serve me, let him follow me; and where I am, there shall also my servant be: if any man serve me, him will my Father honour." (John 12: 25-26)* The calling is clear, the message is dear, and the Lord is always near. You can't beat that with any other Christian form of serving God. All are necessary, but one that starts it all is Salvation first.

So our commission is constructed of power, authority, and a life-changing message that is free. Yes, the gospel of Salvation is free because Jesus paid it all. How hard would it be if a rich man gave you a case of $100 bills and all you had to do is give them away? You might be tempted to keep them for yourself. Many saved people do just that; they do not want to share. The right decision is easy if you see the whole commission as the opportunity to help someone for eternity. Great joy you will bring into their life, not to mention in your life, as the soul-winner!

"Soul Winning IS THE main business of a Christian. The saving of sinners is the thing nearest to the heart of God. For that purpose, Christ came to the earth, and lived and died and rose again. Even now, the angels in Heaven rejoice more over one sinner that repents than ninety-nine just persons that need no repentance. Soul winning is the eternal business. One sows now, and then reaps throughout the endless ages of glory, when he gives the gospel to sinners." (John R. Rice) [3]

Wisdom from Jesus

Realize that people are lost and we know the way. *"I am the way, the truth, and the life: no man cometh unto the Father, but by me." (John 14:6)* We know Jesus is the only truth, the only way, and the only shepherd that has compassion on the lost world. *"But when he saw the multitudes, he was moved with compassion on them, because they fainted, and were scattered abroad, as sheep having no shepherd. Then saith he unto his disciples, The harvest truly is plenteous, but the labourers are few; Pray ye therefore the Lord of the harvest, that he will send labourers into his harvest." (Mat. 9:36-38)* We can't just sit on the side-lines and sing praises when precious souls are in the balance.

How many people die in the U.S. alone or even around the world? The only one that truly knows is God. But, he sees a harvest, a multitude, that lives this life believing a lie from the enemy, going into a Christ-less Hell forever. Is your name in the Lamb's Book of Life? Are you saved, covered by the blood, forgiven of all sins, born again, all things are new? Then your name is there. Others are not as fortunate, *"And whosoever was not found written in the book of life was cast into the lake of fire." (Rev. 20:15)*

"And there shall in no wise enter into it anything that defileth, neither whatsoever worketh abomination or maketh a lie: but they which are written in the Lamb's book of life." (Rev. 21:27)

We can assure ourselves that God sees all humanity as the field for harvest and heaven the destination, whereas Paul explains it as the third heaven in II Corinthians 12:1. He goes to say in verse 4 how a man was, *"caught up into paradise, and heard unspeakable words, which it is not*

3 John R. Rice, THE SOUL-WINNERS FIRE, The Sword of the Lord Publishing, 21,60

lawful for a man to utter." "But as it is written, Eye hath not seen, nor ear heard, neither have entered into the heart of man, the things which God hath prepared for them that love him." (I Cor. 2:9)

What a wonderful thought to know our final destination will be in a place where we will see our loved ones who have gone before us, and we will see the Lord Jesus Christ who died for us and gave us passage for all eternity. Jesus states, *"In my Father's house are many mansions: if it were not so, I would have told you. I go to prepare a place for you And if I go and prepare a place for you, I will come again, and receive you unto myself; that where I am, there ye may be also." (John 14:2-3)* What is interesting about the next verse, in John 14:4, *Jesus said, "And whither I go ye know, and the way ye know."* What exactly does Jesus mean here? How should disciples know about heaven?

We will have to go back to I Corinthians 2 to investigate this matter starting in verse 4, *"And my speech and my preaching was not with enticing words of man's wisdom, but in demonstration of the Spirit and of power."*

Two things to point out here:

> ➤ Man's wisdom will entice listeners.
> ➤ Paul neglected this wisdom to make it clear that the Spirit has the power.

In verse 5, Paul states, *"That your faith should not stand in the wisdom of men, but in the power of God."* What wisdom is he talking about? Verse 7 opens up another interesting and curious statement; *"But we speak the wisdom of God in a mystery, even the hidden wisdom, which God ordained before the world unto our glory."*

The Greek word for wisdom here is *"sofia,"* meaning insight, skill, and intelligence. This word has the same meaning as the Old Testament word for *"wise", "chakam,"* skillful, intelligent, shrewd; and the word *"wisdom", "chakmah,"* Jesus' disciples were endued with this insight. *"The fruit of the righteous is a tree of life; and he that winneth souls is wise."* (Prov. 11:30) So that makes a soul-winner endued with Godly wisdom. I truly believe this wisdom is spiritual and given to all that are saved. Salvation is the catalyst given by the Holy Spirit that starts the experience. When a person accepts Christ, the Word of God, the Spirit of God, and your repented heart and soul meet simultaneously to bring new life that includes wisdom, truth, discernment of light and darkness, and the spiritual insight to know the Father, the Son, and the Holy Spirit. *"The Spirit itself beareth witness with our spirit, that we are the children of God."* (Rom. 8:16)

The Old Testament and Soul-Winning

What is amazing is that soul-winning did not start in the New Testament Church, but in the Old Testament. You may have noticed how Proverbs 11:30 first speaks of the righteous having fruit that sustains life, "The Tree of Life", and the thought here, not to the tree of knowledge, but to life; and most importantly, to Revelation 22:2, where it stands near the "River of Life" in heaven where there is no more curse. (Rev. 22:3)

Restoration is the thought here as well as Psalm 126:6, *"He that goeth forth and weepeth, bearing precious seed, shall doubtless come again with rejoicing, bringing his sheaves with him."* Israel has returned from exile to their homeland out of captivity with tears and joy. How much more is eternal existence than physical?

The Lord wants to set every soul free from the captivity of the enemy, but people are in bondage of sin and blindness from Satan. *"In whom the god of this world hath blinded the minds of them which believe not, lest the light of the glorious gospel of Christ, who is the image of God, should shine unto them." (II Cor. 4:4)* But II Corinthians 4:3 states, *"But if our gospel be hid, it is hid to them that are lost."*

In John 4:37-38, the Bible is referring to labourers from the past when this is stated, *"And herein is that saying true, One soweth, and another reapeth. I sent you to reap that whereon you bestowed no labour: other men labored, and ye are entered into their labours."* No doubt Jesus is referring to someone who existed before his present disciples, sowing seeds at some time in history such as Moses, Daniel, David, Isaiah, etc. about the future Messianic fulfillments. *"...Lift up your eyes, and look on the fields; for they are white already to harvest." (John 4:35)*

Wisdom is Needed

Who are those qualified for this great opportunity? The ones who are "wise."

"All godly wisdom begins with reverence – an understanding of who our sovereign, almighty God is, and out of that understanding, surrendering one's will and behavior to him. There is no alternative foundation on which genuine wisdom can be built. A person may say, 'Do you mean to tell me that with all of my education and experience, I cannot be wise if I don't receive God's forgiveness for my sin and factor God into my life?' That's exactly what I mean to tell you! And I say this not out of my own human understanding – that's what the Word of God says, Apart from God, a human being cannot function in wisdom."(Charles Stanley) 4

To review this qualification, we must remember that the enemy is not going to allow anyone to trespass on his territory. But, the wise are endued with clear orders to march forth, "Go Ye Therefore" with authority, power, and

4 Charles Stanley, *Walking Wisely*, Thomas Nelson Publishers, pg.16

a message. Proverbs 2:10-11 states, *"When wisdom entereth into thine heart, and knowledge is pleasant unto thy soul: Discretion shall preserve thee, understanding shall keep thee."* Please take into account that the task is not easy, but necessary. When we are equipped by Almighty God and have the right attitude of going out to share God's gift of the gospel, nothing will be able to keep us back from this pleasant and privileged opportunity.

What in the world is missing today? Servants of God that will finish the work already started by those who came before us, and sow a new ground for those who come after us.
"And he that reapeth receiveth wages, and gathereth fruit unto life eternal: that both he that soweth and he that reapeth may rejoice together." (John 4:36)

Chapter Two

A Word to the Wise from the Heart

There seems to be a phenomenon happening in our New Testament churches today. The old traditional type of churches are pretty much at a stand - still or dying off as the "New Style " church is exploding with attendance and new ministries with all manner of communication to young people and families. Many of the older Christians have realized that they need to go along with this new venue or be left behind. It seems that reaching people is the main thrust and motive, and many are very successful in this new postmodern era.

But there is a phenomenon going on inside of all this victory. There aren't people walking the aisles to the altar for Salvation like there used to be in the old days. What is going on when the seats are packed, the praises are genuine, and the preaching seems to be on target? The one thing that is obvious to the wise, is the lack of power from on high that moves the church with new life, new decisions, people getting saved and giving their life to the Lord Jesus Christ, then a decision to be baptized.

The older crowd seems to be stuck spiritually, not moved to progress forward. Casual Christianity is just not enough to put the fire back into their hearts. A good Evangelist will come along and skillfully and wisely use the leverage of the Word of God and the Holy Spirit to temporarily put some back on track. But, now the new crowd will only know what they are being taught and experiencing currently in the "New Style" church and not know the true calling. *"Having a form of godliness, but denying the power thereof: from such turn away." (II Tim. 3:5), "Ever learning, and never able to come to the knowledge of the truth." (II Tim. 3:7)*

Spiritual Awakening

The undeniable foundation of Salvation has to be the priority because there is no spiritual life without the Holy Spirit. People can't read the Bible and make any sense, start their Christian growth, get close to God, or be a genuine fire-breathing, soul-winning champion that is much needed today. The Bible does not make it difficult; *"For whosoever shall call upon the name of the Lord shall be saved."(Rom. 10:13)*

We can't ignore the fact that the undertaking of offering Salvation to the lost world is not so easy. So this duty is the one that gets passed on to someone else, like the old adage of, "somebody will do the work, but nobody showed up." The wise can still see that there is no external difference being made, to put it frankly, nobody got saved.

So how do Christians digest this obvious fact? In two ways:

- ➢ Pretend that the job is getting done because I am not qualified to do this kind of serving.
- ➢ Let the church service mask the obligation by getting more sensational with louder music, more programs, and sincere gratitude.

The question still is at hand; are we moving away from soul-winning and Salvation today or are we moving toward our "Great Commission?" If revival is to come, then who is really involved? *"For we wrestle not against flesh and blood, but against principalities, against powers, against the rulers of the darkness of this world, against spiritual wickedness in high places." (Eph.6:12)*

To keep all New Testament Churches today in check with the church's agenda is to have a Salvation barometer visible to all as a reminder of the priority of the church that Jesus died for on the cross. Something to show the church is keeping his purpose in mind, to protect from wrong intentions and perversions creeping in unaware to turn the church worldly and of no effect.

"Love not the world, neither the things that are in the world. If any man love the world, the love of the Father is not in him. For all that is in the world, the lust of the flesh, and the lust of the eyes, and the pride of life, is not of the Father, but of the world." (I John 2:15-16) "And having an high priest over the house of God; Let us draw near with a true heart in full assurance of faith, having our hearts sprinkled from an evil conscience, and our bodies washed with pure water. Let us hold fast the profession of our faith without wavering; (for he is faithful that promised;) And let us consider one another to provoke unto love and to good works: Not forsaking the assembling of ourselves together, as the manner of some is; but exhorting one another: and so much the more, as ye see the day approaching." (Heb. 10:21-25)

All the songs we sing and all the prayers we pray,
Just make the enemy sneer,
But when we win a soul for Jesus Christ,
It makes him tremble and fear.

A spiritual presence of being a lighthouse to the public for those who are earnestly seeking God is the idea. *"Ye are the light of the world. A city that is set on an hill cannot be hid." (Mat. 5:14)* The same goes for the church. Will genuine conversion be found there when the lost visit your church?

Consider the Heart

Every human being has a heart, saved or lost, all are included. This consideration is a double-edged sword because we have an imperfect person trying to win another imperfect person. The only difference is that the witness is generated by the Holy Spirit with built-in love and purpose of God at hand. Jeremiah 17:9 states, *"The heart is deceitful above all things, and desperately wicked: who can know it?"* Saying, this is a warning on how Satan works on both parties through the Salvation process.
He knows as well as God that:
- ❖ The Heart is complicated and can't be trusted
  - o We are born with a sin nature – Rom. 5:19
  - o We have learned how to keep our true feelings in – John 2:25
  - o We are all guilty of sin, we have done the same as the lost person – Rom. 3:23

Defusing your power to witness is the enemy's intention and hopefully you will not let anything penetrate your heart to any life changing decisions. (By the way, church members will be on the fence because of their heart's condition also, and be reluctant to join any soul-winning effort of their church.)

- ❖ Imaginations come from the Heart
  - o Foolishness – Eccl. 8:11
  - o Madness – Eccl. 9:3
  - o Depravity – Jer. 17:9
  - o Extortion and excess – Mat. 23:25
  - o Evil – Mark. 7:21-23
  - o Source of unbelief and covetousness – Heb. 3:12, II Pet. 2:14

I would like to point out at this time that Satan's knowledge is limited. He sees the downside and destruction of everything. After all, isn't he our defeated foe? He can't see the whole picture. He thinks he still has a fighting chance; remember he is a supplanter not the owner of this world.

God's wisdom can't be explained by man or understood; *"O the depths of the riches both of the wisdom and knowledge of God! how unsearchable are his judgments, and his ways past finding out!" (Rom. 11:33)* God's wisdom is amazing in that he knows and can see the sphere of mankind in all directions simultaneously. The witness just gets a portion of God's perspective to fulfill his opportunity to serve him. How privileged we are considering that our eyes have been opened to the truth.

God can use our hearts for his wisdom according to Proverbs 2:10-11, *"When wisdom entereth into thine heart, and knowledge is pleasant unto thy soul; Discretion shall preserve thee, understanding shall keep thee."*

- ❖ The Heart is the Center of Your Life.
    - o The heart needs to be guarded to make the right decisions – Prov. 4:23
    - o The heart controls what we say – Luke 6:45
    - o Salvation comes from the heart – Rom. 10:10
- ❖ The Layers of the heart are only seen by God. – Jer. 17:10
    - o Your integrity will be tested.
    - o When you are being corrupt your actions will show lack of caring
    - o God will give as much grace accordingly

- He will drive the reins of your heart if you let him
❖ God Will Renew Your Heart.
  - Fix your heart upon the Lord – Psa. 112:7, 57:7
  - God's intention is to build your heart – Jer. 24:4-7, Ezek. 11:19-20
  - The heart has to be receptive – Luke 8:15
  - The whole heart is required – Deut. 6:5, Psa. 119:2, Prov. 3:5, Joel 12:12-13

The whole purpose of changing your heart's condition is to be usable of God to change those around you.

I don't think you can find a better example in the Bible than Saul of Tarsus in Acts 9. In verse 9:1, he was breathing out threatening and slaughter, then he met Jesus in verses 2-5, then in verse 6; *"And he trembling and astonished said, Lord what will thou have me to do?"*

The first thing that Saul sought was to serve the Lord, but then in I Corinthians 9:27, we read that he feared that, *"...lest that by any means, when I have preached to others, I myself should be a castaway."* We know that never happened to him because of his new heart condition.

Another good example would be Isaiah in chapter 6 when he saw the vision of the Lord and cried, *"...Woe is me! for I am undone; because I am a man of unclean lips, and I dwell in the midst of a people of unclean lips..."* His quest according to verse 10, *"Make the heart of this people fat, and make their ears heavy, and shut their eyes; lest they see with their eyes, and hear with their ears, and understand with their heart, and convert, and be healed."* Some would look at his message as a privilege; in other words, their hearts were opened as others were provoked.

In Conclusion

The Apostle Paul writes to his co-labourers in I Corinthians 3:18-21, of the conceit that will turn our wisdom futile if we are not careful. *"Let no man deceive himself. If any man among you seemeth to be wise in this world, let him become a fool, that he may be wise. For the wisdom of this world is foolishness with God. For it is written, He taketh the wise in their own craftiness. And again, The Lord knoweth the thoughts of the wise, that they are vain. Therefore let no man glory in men. For all things are yours."*

You can make sure that the Greatest Opportunity in the world will be conducted with the right heart and wisdom if we do it all for Christ. After all, didn't he do it all for us? We don't have to look at the world hopelessly, but with spiritual courage.

The world may be spiraling out of control, but someone has to intervene with a strong and mighty power from the heart of God. *"And the peace of God, which passeth all understanding, shall keep your hearts and minds through Christ Jesus."* (Phil. 4:7)

Chapter Three

What are We Fighting For?

There's going to be a fight, otherwise the Bible wouldn't tell us to, *"Put on the whole armour of God, that ye may be able to stand against the wiles of the devil." (Eph. 6:11)* But the prior verse assures us, *"Finally, my brethren, be strong in the Lord, and in the power of his might." (Eph. 6:10)* If God is on our side, who can stand against us? We have to claim this promise and live it.

Our world is under the curse, we are human beings born physically weak and depraved in a world that seems to want to kill us. Ever been on a cold day at the dusk of the day and see the sun shine beautifully in temperatures that are deadly? We humans find ourselves in a survival mode to stay warm and safe. How can the environment be so unbearable? The same as the flow of the curse, we are up against a world system that is moving with a strong current. To go against the flow will take special conditions to be able to advance. Observe how little fish can survive at the ocean's floor where our man-made submarines can't go because of the immense pressure. How can a little skinny fish survive with all that outside pressure? The answer is that he has an inside pressure pushing out continuously as his environment is pushing in. I say all this to point out that the Holy Spirit in you is greater than any outside obstacle; *"...because greater is he that is in you, than he that is in the world." (I John 4:4)*

Holy Spirit's Mission

The ministry of the Holy Spirit today has more to do with equipping the saints than anything else. He first wants to help us realize his heavenly purpose.
His purpose is to:
- ❖ Possess Us – Rom. 6:4-7
- ❖ Sanctify Us – Rom. 6:13-18
- ❖ Edify Christ – Rom. 6:8-12

We can see here in the book of Romans chapter 6, that the flesh is our weakness. He wants to be a cleansing agent, a positioning agent, and a glorifying agent. *"Howbeit when he, the Spirit of truth, is come, he will guide you into all truth: for he shall not speak of himself; but whatsoever he shall hear, that shall he speak: and he will shew you things to come. He shall glorify me: for he shall receive of mine, and shall shew it unto you." (John 16:13-14)* The Holy Spirit has placed this awareness within us.

The Christian will have to deal with a known condition among servants; "Apprehensive state of Obedience to God." In definition, this means to follow but not be sure, spirit led but not sold out. Romans 7:14-25, the law of the flesh and sin and the struggles thereof, sums this condition up pretty efficiently. (To do or not to do, and how to do that is good, that is the question.)

How does the flesh seem to get the victory more times than we want? We act as if we have the "Natural Mind" that is described in I Corinthians 2:14, *"But the natural mind receiveth not the things of the Spirit of God: for they are foolishness unto him: neither can he know them, because they are spiritually discerned."* We have a self-awareness of putting personal needs first.

Then we have also the "Spiritual Mind" found in Ephesians 4:23-24, *"And be renewed in the spirit of your mind; And that ye put on the new man, which after God is created in righteousness and true holiness."* Has God-awareness, putting his will first. So the fight starts with ourselves to let God lead us without the flesh interfering and getting the victory.

We are a three part person:

- ❖ The Spirit – pneuma
- ❖ The Soul – psuche
- ❖ The Body – soma

When we are using only two parts of who God made us to be, we are not following the Holy Spirit. These two parts or dimensions are the soul and the body, and without the spirit, we become as a common lost person or the unbeliever that has never been regenerated by the Holy Spirit (saved) and can't follow God.

The dimensions of the lost are:

- o The Soul – the mind, will, and emotions
- o The Body – the sinful flesh

A saved person has the capability to serve God because of spirituality; he is connected to God. The trichotomy has three dimensions that should work together. The natural man shuns the spiritual part that connects to God. *"But the natural man receiveth not the things of the Spirit of God: for they are foolishness unto him: neither can he know them, because they are spiritually discerned." (I Cor.2:14)*

Who is Your Authority?

Even though the saved person is connected to God, he doesn't always take advantage of this privilege and doesn't always listen to God. Let me explain by going back to the Garden of Eden. Adam and Eve were connected to God in every way with their minds innocent and oblivious to anything else but God. But God has given mankind a free will to serve him or not, so when the tempter, old serpent, came along with the attitude to entice Eve, then Adam, and was successful, sin came into this world and the "dis-connect" began. They ran from God and hid themselves.

The first sign that God had not moved and wanted to communicate with his creation is found in Genesis 3:9; *"And the Lord God called unto Adam, and said unto him, Where art thou?"* Of course we know Adam and Eve were afraid of God (3:10) when they hid themselves. The curse of the earth and the terminable life had begun. Mankind started using their soul and body as their main function if they chose not to include God or his instruction in their lives.

The "dis-connect" is there, but God has not closed the channel of communication with man. All we have to do is call upon the name of the Lord and "re-connect" on a daily basis. (Phil. 4:6, Prov. 2:1-9) If we don't "re-connect" our spirit with God through the Holy Spirit, the enemy will come and intercept, sending us back to the two dimensional soul and body way of thinking. He can't change who we are, saved believer in Christ, but he can tempt us to not listen or include God in our day, thus sending the soul the message to do your own will not God's will.

Think of this process as a structure of an owner, manager, and an employee.

"The Paradigm of Authority"

- ❖ The Owner – Spirit
    - o The Spirit of God will instruct. Who are you listening to, the Holy Spirit or Satan? If we don't pray and give this Authority to God, Satan will intercept.
- ❖ The Manager – Soul
    - o Will follow orders from the Owner. Who did we give Authority to and take orders

from? If not God, Satan has now intercepted and the soul will make wrong decisions.

❖ The Employee – Body
  o Will follow orders from the Manager. The Manager is making wrong decisions because he is following the wrong Authority. The flesh will now sin.

Soul Control

"For what is a man profited, if he shall gain the whole world, and lose his own soul? or what shall a man give in exchange for his soul?" (Mat. 16:26) The word "lose" in the Greek is the word "zemioo" which means to injure, detriment, or damage. The very implication of the soul being the mind, will, and emotions can be controlled; consider a "Soul Control." Just because you are saved does not mean that the devil can't tempt you into sinning. Again, how does this happen? By by-passing God's Wisdom and Authority through his Spirit and rely on the Soul's instructions, which are wrong because of Satan's interception. Now you are relying on man's wisdom that can't serve God on his terms. The choice is ours, serve God or our selves.

The Apostle Paul instructed the brethren at Thessalonica in his first letter, chapter 5:16-24, "Rejoice evermore. Pray without ceasing. In everything give thanks: for this the will of God in Christ Jesus concerning you. Quench not the Spirit. Despise not prophesyings. Prove all things; hold fast that which is good. Abstain from all appearance of evil. And the very God of peace sanctify you wholly; and I pray God your whole spirit and soul and body be preserved *blameless unto the coming of our Lord Jesus Christ. Faithful is he that calleth you, who also will do it."*

The battle is on for the soul, including yours, because we are vulnerable and live in a sinful world with a fallen agenda. We need to consider our soul's condition each day. What are we fighting for? In priority, the fight is of our own faithfulness to the Lord. The wise will understand what is at stake here and take these things seriously. The longer that you have been in the battle over the soul, the more wisdom you have to understand the "Whole Armour of God." (Eph. 6) As God exhorted Joshua; *"... Be strong and of a good courage; be not afraid, neither be thou dismayed: for the Lord thy God is with thee withersoever thou goest." (Josh. 1:9)* Take this encouragement to the heart.

When we accept Christ by the Holy Spirit and the Word of God, we will continue to experience confusing thoughts in our mind, will, and emotions. But, now the Holy Spirit and the Word of God make it possible to *"Be transformed by the renewing of our mind..." (Rom.12:2)* This will take saturation by meditation and memorization of the scriptures.

Meditate on This

"This book of the Law shall not depart out of thy mouth; but thou shalt meditate therein day and night;... for then thou shalt make thy way prosperous, and then thou shalt have good success." (Josh. 1:8) Saturation is just what it sounds like, to be covered with a substance until you and the substance unite. What we truly want to do is to push out of our minds anything that does not coincide with scripture. We have built a thought structure our whole lives that mainly has dictated our direction and decisions. But, where has that gotten you so far? An unsaved person is separated from God with a wide margin of error. It seems

that some are fundamentally opposed to anything that even speaks of God. You will have to choose some major changes, such as; friends, jobs, places, etc.

Your walk will change if you desire to be Godly. *"Blessed is the man that walketh not in the counsel of the ungodly, nor standeth in the way of sinners, nor sitteth in the seat of the scornful. But his delight is in the law of the Lord; and in his law doth he meditate day and night. And he shall be like a tree planted by the rivers of water, that bringeth forth his fruit in his season; his leaf also shall not wither; and whatsoever he doeth shall prosper." (Psa. 1:1-3)* Our goal is to be like that tree planted strategically to be nurtured from the life source, so we can grow and bring forth fruit.

Start with memorization of whole thoughts and passages such as: Jesus – John 1, Salvation – Romans 10, Faith – James 1&2, Love - I Corinthians 13, The Flesh – Romans 6, Wisdom – Proverbs, etc. You can realize your personal weaknesses and start memorization and meditation on these passages to strengthen your resolve, and you will see a reshaping of your thoughts saturating your mind, will, and emotions (soul). Yes, being saved is just the foundation and now the structure has got to be built. God's character with a Godly purpose doesn't happen by chance. *"Study to shew thyself approved unto God, a workman that needeth not to be ashamed, rightly dividing the word of truth." (II Tim. 2:15)*

Pierce the Darkness

"For we wrestle not against flesh and blood, but against principalities, against powers, against the rulers of darkness of this world, against spiritual wickedness in high places. Wherefore take unto you the whole armour of God, that ye may be able to withstand in the evil day, and having done all, to stand." (Eph. 6:12-13) Let's realize that we

have to be prepared to stand as we withstand. The devil has a host of fallen angels in his regiment instructed to prevent anyone from crossing the threshold of Salvation. It is a great struggle to pull a soul over to the light from a blinded state.

Most people don't think that there are any consequences or judgments in this life because they are really hopelessly blind. Notice the words of Isaiah 59:9-10, *"Therefore is judgement far from us, neither doth justice overtake us: we wait for light, but behold obscurity; for brightness, but we walk in darkness. We grope for the wall like the blind, and we grope as if we had no eyes: we stumble at noon-day as in the night; we are in desolate places as dead men."* The truth is that God designed us with himself in mind. There is a part of us that feels the need for life and if not regenerated, we continue to walk among the dead. This is the spirit of man that needs God to fill the void that God has left open. *"For what man knoweth the things of a man, save the spirit of man which is in him?" (I Cor. 2:11)*

This condition is not permanent because the devil is not our real god. *"But if our gospel be hid, it is hid to them that are lost: in whom the god of this world hath blinded the minds of them which believe not, lest the light of the glorious gospel of Christ, who is the image of God, should shine unto them." (II Cor. 4:3-4)* The only way to pierce the darkness is with the gospel of truth. *"Ye are the light of the world." (Mat. 5:14)* Paul's mission was to be a light unto the Gentiles, found in Acts 13:47, *"...I have set thee to be a light of the Gentiles, that thou shouldest be for salvation unto the ends of the earth."*

No matter to whom you are witnessing, the spiritual boundaries are set. The curse on one side includes people that are lost, clouded by darkness, leaning to worldly wisdom, promoting humanity and fleshly ideas, in which the ends thereof are the ways of death. This eternal separation from God is Hell. The threshold unto eternal life is the spiritual battle ground. This middle ground is discouraged by the enemy because this is where the lost souls are won over to God's side. *"Behold, I stand at the door (threshold), and knock: if any man hear my voice, and open the door, I will come into him, and will sup with him, and he with me." (Rev. 3:20)* You will find that many people are in this threshold and are seeking for answers and truth. The Holy Spirit is already working on them and their hesitant hearts.

It reminds me of the "great gulf fixed" in Luke 16 when the rich man begged for comfort from the torment that he was experiencing. Abraham said, *"... Between us and you there is a great gulf fixed: so that they which would pass from hence to you cannot; neither can they pass to us, that would come from thence."* This is speaking of a permanent setting, where now we have a "great opportunity" to lead them to the Heavenly side, where the soul is set free and their name is written in the Lamb's Book of Life.

Consider the curse as a cocoon shrouding a person into a helpless estate until the metamorphosis takes place. The great awakening of their soul hasn't happened. The change can take place, the creator intended for it, but the subject lies dormant until a miracle breaks them out of this condition. The Word of God and the Spirit of God provide the miracle. Once the person hears the Word and ponders the thoughts in their heart and mind, the Holy Spirit takes over. This is worth fighting for; God can use you to make this miracle happen. *"We have also a more sure word of prophecy; whereunto ye do well that ye take heed, as unto a light that shineth in a dark place, until the day dawn, and the day star arise in your hearts." (II Peter 1:19)*

"It is impossible for any man or woman who is following Christ to walk in darkness. If there is a soul here in the darkness, groping in the fog and the midst of the earth, let me tell him it is because he has got away from the true light. There is nothing but light that will dispel darkness. So let those who are walking in spiritual darkness admit Christ in their hearts. He is the Light." (D.L. Moody)

Chapter Four

It's a Matter of Life or Death

Where do you go when you die? This question is probably the most asked question among children and adults. When a child asks an adult, the answer seems rather pat; you go to Heaven to live with God and all the angels. If a loved one dies, everyone wants to think that is where they are, living a better life with no more pain, and we will see them again one day if we are a good person, maybe go to church, and be kind, loving, and generous. When at a funeral, I have never heard anyone get up and do the eulogy and explain why this person is in Hell today. It is either, they don't know for sure, or they surely are in Heaven. *"If a man die, shall he live again? all the days of my appointed time will I wait, till my change come." (Job 14:14)* Back in verse 10, Job asks another question, *"But man dieth, and wasteth away: yea, man giveth up the ghost, and where is he?"* The book of Hebrews has the answer: *"And as it is appointed unto men once to die, but after this the judgment." (Heb. 9:27)*

In times before the cross and the resurrection of Jesus Christ, all the dead went to a place named "sheol" in the Hebrew, meaning grave. Job saw this as a mysterious place because you can clearly see by his questions that he did not understand life and death entirely. The only hope he encountered was to think of a possible resurrection. His living conditions, as God put him through the great test, put him in a life or death situation. Most people don't really consider these most major questions until illness or old age has come upon them. *"O my God! It is over. I have come to the end of it – the end, the end. To have only one life, and to have done with it! To have lived and loved, and triumphed, and now to know it is over! One may defy everything else but this."* *(Queen Elizabeth I)*

Mankind lives in a state of euphoria to the degree that we die, but that is an unspeakable subject matter. So with all the thoughts of such a vulnerable position they will not bring themselves to that crossroads mentally or emotionally. Living forever is the only good thought and don't bring me down otherwise with all that talk about Heaven or Hell. But in the back of their minds, the thought is there because God put it there in all living souls. The creator has claimed the souls, *"Behold, all souls are mine; as the soul of the father, so also the soul of the son is mine: the soul that sinneth, it shall die."* *(Ezek. 18:4)* We live with a false sense of security; a pretense of self-existence. The truth is, we had nothing to do with being born and God will determine when we die. The devil would like to build us up with pride and self-worth, and even use our God-given abilities to further propagate his agenda.

It is easy to accept the existence of Heaven, but not so accepting when it comes to the existence of Hell. The New Testament name for Hell is "hades," the place of departed souls, and "ghehennah," the place of everlasting punishment. Jesus gave us a brief description in Mark 9:44, *"Where their worm dieth not, and the fire is not quenched."* That doesn't sound like "soul sleep" or a non-existence to me, but a real place where the sinning soul is forever separated into a state of torment. *"And it came to pass, that the beggar died, and was carried by the angels into Abraham's bosom: the rich man also died, and was buried; And in hell he lift up his eyes, being in torments,* and seeth Abraham afar off, and Lazarus in his bosom. And he cried and said, Father Abraham, have mercy on me, and send Lazarus, that he may dip the tip of his finger in water, and cool my tongue; for I am tormented in this flame."(Luke 16:22-24)* "...to be absent from the body, and to be present with the Lord." (II Cor. 5:8)* This is a state of being that all mankind has to accept. Just because the person in the body dies, the soul is still eternal and is going to exist in a state of heavenly glory or a separated torment in Hell.

As you may have noticed, the beggar and Abraham are in a place that had no torment, but rather a place that is deemed safe; a place called "paradise." The term "paradise," "paradeisos" is the name of the current destination of the saints. Jesus promised the thief on the cross this place, *"Verily I say unto thee, To day shalt thou be with me in paradise." (Luke 23:43)* Paul mentions the third Heaven in II Corinthians chapter 12 as a place where you are caught up. He could not tell if he was out of the body or in the body, but a man was caught up into this "paradise." *"And I knew such a man, (whether in the body, or out of the body, I cannot tell: God knoweth;) How that he was caught up into paradise, and heard unspeakable words, which it is not lawful for a man to utter." (II Cor. 12:3-4)* The same word is used in Rev. 2:7, *"He that hath an ear, let him hear what the Spirit saith unto the churches; To him that overcometh will I give to eat of the tree of life, which is in the midst of the paradise of God."* All of these occasions agree that there is a Heaven that awaits the soul that is saved.

The Wall of Communication

There is a great opportunity to lead people to the cross before death or rapture comes. But the steps of victory seem a bit steep, to take someone not believing in God to saved and ready for Heaven. Paul could feel the challenge and was willing to take it on when he wrote; *"To the weak became I as weak, that I might gain the weak: I am made*

all things to all men, that I might by all means save some."
(I Cor. 9:22)

How do you reach people with the gospel? We have to graciously love them to the cross. The challenge is how much do you care about their lost and hopeless condition? People live in a world that pushes, dictates, and demands as the soul of the unsaved has created a defense mechanism to put up a barrier to ward off undesirable communication. In other words, people are pretty much closed off to the truth. You can't force someone to accept Christ as their savior, it has to be their choice.

The "ground" of the heart has to be sowed and cultivated first. Let's go through seven steps of the common person that needs Jesus Christ as savior or they will die in a Christ-less torment in Hell.

The soul-winner will observe:
1. Doesn't believe in God – defiant
   - doesn't care about right or wrong
   - religion is a crutch
   - to each their own
2. Doesn't sin – as good as anyone else
   - I am a good person
   - I will give to charities
3. Loves life the way it is – flesh comes first
   - I will find all the pleasures
   - the world's agenda is fine with me
4. Decided that churches are controlling
   - all they want is my money
   - they also want my time
5. Heard of Jesus and Heaven
   - not in church
   - believes in God

6. Been thinking about going to church
    - not convinced I need to
    - no real convictions
    - wants to go to heaven
7. Ready to be saved
    - ripe to the point of listening
    - the heart is open to the truth
    - need some answers

You can observe when you talk to someone about their spiritual condition about where they stand according to these steps to Heaven. It will take a special kind of person to step up and meet the challenge of leading them to the Salvation step.

The Bible calls this our "fruit." *"The fruit of the righteous is a tree of life; and he that winneth souls is wise." (Prov. 11:30)* The Hebrew word for fruit is, "periy" (per-ee) meaning reward, and the Greek word, found in many places, is "karpos" meaning as plucked up; *"Say not ye, there are yet four months, and then cometh harvest? behold, I say unto you, Lift up your eyes, and look on the fields; for they are white already to harvest. And he that reapeth receiveth wages, and gathereth fruit unto life eternal: that both he that soweth and he that reapeth may rejoice together." (John 4:35-36)*

The Seeds are Sown

The whole thought of soul-winning is to enter the field where you see seeds of the Word of God has been sown and sprouting up in men's hearts, and where the Word of God has not been sown and is very needed. The fruit doesn't come quickly if you ask a farmer, but Jesus is pointing out in John 4:38, *"I sent you to reap that whereon ye bestowed no labour: other men laboured, and ye are entered into their labours."* The work has started and needs finished. Your forefathers started the great churches that we have to keep going.

Our world today has more technology and media opportunities than ever before with online Bible, Christian commercials, and Christian cinema. The seeds have been planted multiple times to a more vast crowd. Christian books offer a gourmet feast on the deeper things of God, but we know the common person would be reluctant to dive into something over their head. In reality, you can't understand the deeper things of God until your eyes have been open to the truth at salvation. So let's go sow the seeds and watch them grow!

The parable of the sower in Matthew 13 will gives us a layout of the field as it has always been and still is today. *"Behold, a sower went forth to sow." (Vs.3)*

(original thought)
Vs. 4 ... some seeds fell by the way side, and the fowls came and devoured them up.
(meaning)
Vs. 19 When any one heareth the word of the kingdom, and understandeth it not, then cometh the wicked one, and catcheth away...

(original)
Vs. 5 Some fell upon stony places, where they had not much earth: and forthwith they sprung up, because they had no deepness of earth.
(meaning)
Vs. 20... the same is he that heareth the word, and anon (soon) with joy receiveth it.

(original)
Vs. 6 And when the sun was up, they were scorched; and because they had no root, they withered away.
(meaning)

Vs. 21 Yet hath he not root in himself, but dureth for a while: for when tribulation or persecution ariseth because of the word, by and by he is offended.

(original)
Vs. 7 And some fell among thorns; and the thorns sprung up, and choked them.
(meaning)
Vs. 22 ...he that heareth the word; and the care of this world, and the deceitfulness of riches, choke the word, and he becometh unfruitful.

(original)
Vs. 8 But other fell into good ground, and brought forth fruit, some an hundredfold, some sixtyfold, some thirtyfold.
(meaning)
Vs.23 ...he that heareth the word, and understandeth it; which also beareth fruit, and bringeth forth, some an hundredfold, some sixty, some thirty.

You see how careful and wise a sower needs to be, because the Word of God works on him as well. At some time, the sower's heart had to be the "good ground" to accept the word, nurture the word, then live out the Word of God. *"For the word of God is quick, and powerful, and sharper than any twoedged sword..." (Heb. 4:12)*

You handle the Word, and the Word will pierce you as well; it seems to be the right and beneficial intention of God. That is the only way to become fruitful.

You will always see potential fruit and wonder why this fruit has no life. The life flow has to be conceived in to even start to become fruitful, in the spiritual sense. The life flow has to become a perpetual motion, or you will see death start occurring.

Church be Aware

Two things that happen in every church; people move away and people die. This will affect the attendance, the offerings, and eventually the condition of the church. We can keep things lively with music, family enrichment, stewardship, building projects, youth programs, senior involvement, missions; but if there is no undercurrent of new life, expressively, new souls saved, the foundation will eventually weaken spiritually. Compromise will become common place, and the focus will shift from the powerful spiritual experience of hearts and lives changed to a church movement of man-made proportions with no clear direction for those, especially the young, that have not seen or experienced all the Spirit can be in God's house.

What will happen if the crop is not harvested on time? The fruit thereof will fall and die with decay because there is no life source feeding into it. All Jesus is saying is that there are those going by the wayside perishing without being cultivated and rescued by the saving, life-giving truth of the Word of God. Somebody will point out that "you can't save them all." That sounds more like an excuse rather than a lament.

"I am the vine, ye are the branches: He that abideth in me, and I in him, the same bringeth forth much fruit: for without me ye can do nothing." (John 15:5) The partnership is vital to the work. We have to rely upon the life source. The same thing is mentioned in John 15:1, with Jesus and the Father; *"I am the true vine, and my Father is the husbandman."* What an opportunity to serve with Jesus, to draw life from Jesus and the Holy Spirit, and to supernaturally save the Hell-bound soul to a victorious soul, inheriting eternal life. You can make a difference of life and death!

Chapter Five

Does Anybody Know the Time?

The most elusive, yet the most used subject ever, is the thought of time. There are many areas in the Bible which time envelops the world we live in, the life we live, the matters of eternity, and the conclusion of all things. God invented time for his purpose. It seems ironic that the thought of time would be considered in the heavens where there are no time constraints. But if we look closely, we will realize that every allotted interval, "chronos" in the Greek, pertains to a matter that affects our world.

There is no beginning or end for the Lord because he is truly the everlasting, and when considering our souls, he has promised us everlasting life. What does this entail? If we had existed before we were born on this earth, we would have experienced eternity past, as well as eternity present, and eternity future. Our everlasting starts when we become a living soul at birth. We know the soul is eternal and will continue on after we die in the body. The question is will we spend eternity in Heaven or Hell? God is not willing that any should perish, but that all should come to repentance according to II Peter 3:9.

Secondly, this planet we live on has a terminal existence in its present condition. *"That in the dispensation of the fulness of times he might gather together in one all things in Christ, both which are in heaven, and which are on earth; even in him."* (Eph.1:10) As John recorded in Revelation 21:1, *"And I saw a new heaven and a new earth: for the first heaven and the first earth were passed away; and there was no more sea."* This earth as we know it is not in its infancy, but is in full maturity today. Like any living organism, there is birth (Genesis 4000 BC), there is a growth period (pre- Bethlehem until 400 BC), and there is maturity, (since Jesus came and ushered in grace from the cross).

We have been living in God's grace with an uncertain ending. *"But of that day and hour knoweth no man, no, not the angels of heaven, but my Father only." (Mat. 24:36)* We are on God's life support and only God the Father will determine when the time is ripe for the final harvest.

In the days of Noah, people were warned of a time when the rains would come, but did not heed the warning or embrace God until it was too late. Again, Matthew 24, "*But as the days of Noe were, so shall also the coming of the Son of man be. For as in the days that were before the flood they were eating and drinking, marrying and giving in marriage, until the day that Noe entered into the ark. And knew not until the flood came, and took them all away; so shall also the coming of the Son of man be." (37-39)* I would like to point out the word "knew" in verse 39 is the Greek word "ginosko," which means to be aware of, have knowledge, perceive, to be sure, to understand. The people lived in the witness of Noah and his family building this slow project and obviously did not take him seriously.

We can look back at this grievous time and feel sorry for all the men, women, and children that lost their lives, but can we see that God showed his grace through it all? The earth was wicked and violent in those days; *"And God saw that the wickedness of man was great in the earth, and that every imagination of the thoughts of his heart was only evil continually. And it repented the Lord that he had made man on the earth, and it grieved him at his heart." (Gen.*

6:5-6)* Verse 8, *"But Noah found grace in the eyes of the Lord."* There was still hope for mankind as this truth still stands today. *"For by grace are ye saved through faith; and that not of yourselves: it is the gift of God."* (Eph. 2:8) Saving grace is only by faith, taking God seriously at his Word. People do not take the "coming of the Son of man," Jesus' return, as the truth, or are they just not well informed? Prophetically speaking, time is running out.

"For the Lord himself shall descend from heaven with a shout, with the voice of the archangel, and with the trump of God: and the dead in Christ shall rise first: then we which are alive and remain shall be caught up together with them in the clouds, to meet the Lord in the air: and so shall we ever be with the Lord. Wherefore comfort one another with these we words." (I Thes. 4:16-18)

Heavy stuff indeed. As those in the days of Noah never saw rain, it was totally unbelievable. When Paul wrote this to the Thessalonian church, they had never seen flight of man, unbelievable for the day. But what is our excuse today? We see space themes all the time on the big screen. The supernatural fills the airwaves today with devils, evil, Armageddon, all with a humanistic twist of real truth. People are aware but desensitized by these displays of falsehood. Unbelievable, will never happen, is the word on the streets and in the common household.

Time has Become Routine

Our time today falls somewhere between the recent past and the future with no urgency to act on much of anything. The routine of our day doesn't seem to be in the chronology at all. Time to get up, time to eat, time to go to work, time to go to school, time for play, time to go to bed, etc., is the real world. The focus on goals is the only real hope to keep people motivated in this mundane routine, "for what is the meaning of it all?" the world asks.

"Motivation is the drive within us, it is that something within us that moves us, stirs us, punches our buttons, gets us moving. Different factors, of course, motivate different people. For example, some people are highly motivated by the approval of others or highly motivated by a sense of position or prominence. Others are motivated by more money; others by their appearance; others by unusual stimuli." 5 *(Charles Stanley)*

To help your fellowman is an added extra activity only to justify your goodness with man and God, and hope it doesn't go unnoticed.

The old story of the frog in the cook pot seems to be coming true in our world today, where we are slowly being boiled to death in a seemingly comfortable warm water. Again the Apostle Paul deals with this complacency in the Ephesian church, found in chapter 5:14-16, *"Wherefore he saith, Awake thou that sleepest, and arise from the dead, and Christ shall give thee light. See then that ye walk circumspectly, not as fools, but as wise. Redeeming the time, because the days are evil."*

The Time is Now

I think everyone agrees that the days are evil with mass shootings, bombings, evil troops moving over the globe trying to control our peaceful world with its devilish agenda. Yes, we can agree on these issues, but we can't agree on a cause or solution to slow down this problem. As Christians, we know that the Spirit of God can come into the lives of any or all of those who will "hear" the Word.

5 Charles Stanley, Confronting Casual Christianity, BROADMAN PRESS, pg. 66

The life changing gospel will turn the events of a city, country, or the entire world. The mission of the soul-winner is to take advantage of this opportunity to reach one soul at a time, that will lead to one family at a time, and impact the community with the Bible-believing perspective on right and wrong; in which God refers to as "sin."

Is the time right to be proactive or reactive? Meaning to try to influence the world with the righteousness of God, or just sit back and accept that the times are foretold to be this way and pray for the safety of all? This reminds us of a day at Sodom and Gomorrah, where they were too afraid to go out at night and stayed behind closed doors.

"To every thing there is a season, and a time to every purpose under the heaven."(Eccl.3:1) "A time to rend, and a time to sew; a time to keep silence, and a time to speak; A time to love, and a time to hate; a time of war, and a time of peace."(Eccl.3:7-8)

Include the time that we are in today and realize this is purposed of God. You can't pick and choose, be selective of one, when we are involved in all.

"But of that day and hour knoweth no man, no, not the angels of heaven, but my father only." (Matt. 24:36) Almighty God has given the allowed time so we can take advantage of leading those we love and those whom he has already touched with his eternal truth. We can't continue to watch seeds go by the wayside by this untoward generation. Our time is now, our harvest is waiting, our victory is for the taking.

The Good Old Days

The coming of Christ is inevitable, as many have preached over the years in this church age. But this age has waxed old and is starting to become complacent. The revival fires of yesteryear have cooled down to a slow ember that is still there, burning, but will soon die out without fanning the flames. Everyone says that the message never grows old and they are correct, but we can't treat our New Testament churches as old photographs in an album, where we look back into it every once in a while, and smile saying, "those were special times." The feeling of our heart just leaps with joy as we gaze upon the past with a little sadness, saying; "those were the good old days."

I remember when people walked down the aisles at the invitation and got saved; accepted Christ as their Savior. The preachers had a message to preach filled with fire and come what may, the service was taken to a spiritual elevation when nobody cared what their schedules were as they witnessed a miracle at the church service. People shouted with passion, got on a roll of excitement, and could not wait until Sunday night service. Men prayed before the service for people to accept Christ. Families needed a godly dad to bring their children to Christ and a good, Godly wife and mother to raise them right. The big event of the week was to go to church and never miss a service. We had "Victory in Jesus, My Savior Forever" and we were "Living on the Mountain Underneath the Cloudless Sky, Praise God!" The anthems of the powerful preaching rang throughout the airwaves and down the streets to break the fog of humanistic, sinful, and worldly existence and changed households for Jesus Christ. Somebody please say "Amen!"

In Times like These

"In times like these, we need a Savior," are ageless words penned by a songwriter that could see the tumultuous world we face today. Be very sure your anchor holds the Solid Rock.

How can people fare the times with hardships of daily lives' challenges and still manage to have a spiritual life that takes priority over anything else? Let's look at the example in Nehemiah 4:17; *"They which builded on the wall, and they that bare burdens, with those that laded, every one with one of his hands wrought in the work, and with the other hand held a weapon."* What does this tell us? The enemy, like Sanbalat and his mocking crew, will always resist you and war with you. It takes a weapon in one hand, the Bible, and a team of builders to accomplish the work. Jesus never sent anyone alone to do the warring against the gates of Hell; this is a group effort. There is more to the spiritual battle than worship and praise, in which we do very well in exhibiting this freedom.

The church effort is to be:

- ➢ Realistic about the times we are living in, (not to candy-coat it)
- ➢ Be aware that the enemy will try to divide the group
- ➢ Be prayerful for the power to witness
- ➢ Regain the power of the Lord Jesus and the Holy Spirit to resist the devil

"I am come to send fire on the earth; and what will I, if it be already kindled?"(Luke 12:49) Only then will we start making a difference; the wall, or our purpose, to plow the field.

"The devil has a fiendishly clever way of sowing tares among the wheat (the church), just as our Lord predicted in His kingdom of heaven parables... The Bible makes it clear that doctrinal confusion will rise to a crescendo in the latter days, leading many to depart from the faith ..." 6

6 Tim LaHaye, Jerry B. Jenkins, *Are We Living in the End Times?*, Tyndale House Publishers, pg. 7

There is apostasy present everywhere, so hold on for extreme resistance because the devil knows his time is short. John gave us this wisdom in I John 2:18; *"Little children, it is the last time: and as ye have heard that antichrist shall come, even now are there many antichrists; whereby we know that it is the last time."* The devil's plan, in these last days, is to pull you away from anything that points to Jesus. Jesus said in John 14:6, *"I am the way, the truth, and the life..."* These are the devil's targets; the "way," another deceitful, worldly belief or self-centered program. The "truth," what is the truth? It was the question posed to Eve. The truth is not a thing, but a person. The "life," he wants to make you think that you can be in control of your own life, while he schedules it out for you little by little. The old saying, *"if you give the devil an inch, he will become a ruler,"* is the plan. What decisions can you make for God while he controls your soul? He doesn't want God in control of your life, so we keep listening to the wrong authority. You are still saved but misdirected, partly by your flesh and mostly by the enemy.

This is why in these times we find it so hard to resist the devil; because he and his helpers are placed in most every area of the current culture of society. The only place safe is the church, right? Not on your life. Some do the devil's bidding in the face of the righteous. The church has become open season on anyone who leans toward the world or any form of compromise. *"Casting all your care upon him; for he careth for you. Be sober, be vigilant; because your adversary the devil, as a roaring lion, walketh about, seeking whom he may devour: Whom resist steadfast in the faith, knowing that the same afflictions are accomplished in your brethren that are in the world. But the God of all grace, who hath called us unto his eternal glory by Christ Jesus, after that ye have suffered a while, make you perfect, stablish, strengthen, settle you." (I Peter 5:7-10)*

It seems that self-absorption is the purpose of the church; what can I get out of the church? When the Lord Jesus Christ gave us the example of the welfare of others; he laid down his life in sacrifice as we should also. *"From whom the whole body fitly joined together and compacted by that which every joint supplieth, according to the effectual working in the measure of every part, maketh increase of the body unto the edifying of itself in love." (Eph. 4:16)*

It is time to keep our minds and hearts on the real issues that face the people today. That always starts with Salvation first. *"Love worketh no ill to his neighbor: therefore love is the fulfilling of the law. And that, knowing the time, that now it is high time to awake out of sleep: for now is our salvation nearer than when we believed. The night is far spent, the day is at hand: let us therefore cast off the works of darkness, and let us put on the armour of light." (Rom. 13:10-12)* The time for rapture and judgment is upon us now and the moments are fleeting. The "greatest opportunity" is Salvation by leading others to the Lord Jesus Christ.

Chapter Six

Here Comes the Judge

I have never met anyone who likes to take tests, unless they have studied the subject thoroughly and can advance because of the results. Accept the fact that there have to be tests regardless of how you feel about it. The schools are required to see what you have learned to promote you to the next level. Some people have no desire to continue their education after high school because of their feeling of being on trial.

Society today has an overall attitude of not wanting to be judged or scrutinized on the job and especially on their own time. People don't want to hear that there are consequences for their actions, but Christians have accepted the fact that sin has to be paid for because sin violates God's word. The very mention of the word "sin" triggers a defensive state of mind. Everyone, the lost and saved alike, knows this word carries consequences.

Sin in the Old Testament refers to a couple of different things; "chata," means to miss the mark and to sin against God. "Chattah," refers to an offense with penalty. The New Testament carries the same meaning with the words "harmartia" and "harmartano," to miss the mark and offense with penalty.

For All Have Sinned

Which brings to light what sin truly is in the presence of a Holy God. We don't measure up as humans with an ever shifting soul that will obey one minute and disobey the next. *"Therefore to him that knoweth to do good, and doeth it not, to him it is sin." (James 4:17)*

Thank God for grace; *"Where sin abounded, grace did much more abound." (Rom. 5:20)* We become our own worst enemy when we think God will always overlook our sin. Our merits don't have anything to do with cancelling sin. You reap what you sow. I get the picture of a child disobeying the Father, getting into trouble, and relying on the Father's mercy to come along and fix the mess he has made. *"I have been good other times, don't that account for something?"* the child cries. Each and every individual sin has to be accounted for. While the Christian struggles with his own flesh on each of these offenses, the lost world has a lifetime of sins weighing them down and forever separating them from Almighty God. We are fortunate that we have accepted Christ, been set free from the penalty of sin, and given grace to try to hit the mark by living a Godly life. *"If we confess our sins, he is faithful and just to forgive us our sins, and to cleanse us from all unrighteousness." (I John 1:9)*

What are the Odds

Nobody knows how long we have on this earth, either death or rapture will occur and the opportunity will be over to witness to that individual who needs Christ. I guarantee if you ask God for someone to witness to, he will answer your prayer promptly because he knows two things:

- ❖ You are willing to serve him in the most important capacity
- ❖ He knows who need saved and how long they have left to live

Ask yourself why Jesus came on this earth to die for mankind. *"For the Son of man is come to seek and to save that which was lost." (Luke 19:10)* He not only paid the penalty for sin; (II Cor. 5:20-21), but he has made the Salvation of the cross a mandate to give all people the opportunity to accept Jesus Christ as savior and close the separation forever.

The only problem is that the world is getting more corrupt under Satan's influence, and people are dying at an alarming rate. Statistics will prove that the world is more populated today than ever before, hence, more people to die by percentage. The world will outnumber the truly born-again Christian ten to one, and the Christian outnumbers the soul-winner ten to one, and to every ten that you witness to, one will be saved. What are the odds? These are realistic, history proven, accepted facts of the odds.

"For the wages of sin is death; but the gift of God is eternal life through Jesus Christ our Lord." (Rom. 6:23) "And as it is appointed unto men once to die, but after this the judgment." (Heb. 9:27) These two verses are the message of truth for the mission. We all die, but we don't all have the same consequences at judgment. The sinner receives his wages after a long life of sin; eternal death, as the ones that have received the gift of God; eternal life. the comparison and choice looks easy, but the lost world has not been told, doesn't believe it, or hasn't thought death through.

God has created a person with a sense of worship to focus on living while still employed with the passion to direct his thoughts on him. We like to replace God's created passion with jobs, sports, hobbies, etc., therefore people will go through life known for the passion or employment that they served, and at the end of their life, what do they have to show for it? There lies a man or woman who excelled in their field and that's all? I say you can excel, and be a Christian (believer) and know where you will spend eternity. I say again, your merits will not cancel out sin. What is not understandable about God wanting you to have passions to a degree in this life and to have Salvation as your eternal security?

The day of judgment is real and inevitable. The saying that, "sinners don't know they are sinning," is unbelievable; it is not that they don't know as much as they don't care. *"I won't be held by consequences,"* or, *"who are you to judge?"* seem to be the most famous replies among the unsaved. So are you saying there is another judge?

Heaven or Hell

Heaven is the place where everyone wants to go, and Hell is full of people with good intentions, or should I say, late intentions or slow to grasp the opportunity. "Get right or get left," is a powerful statement that does not only apply to rapture. You will not be able to decide your eternity after you die. If you could, it would be very clear what your decision would be. As the rich man that died in Luke 16; *"and in hell he lift up his eyes, being in torments ..."* He was very aware of where he was as the consequences of his sinful life revealed itself. There was no party with friends or anything there to comfort him for all of eternity.

I have heard some say that Hell is here on earth. But they could not be more incorrect:
- ➤ Christians exist here, there are none in Hell
- ➤ I can quench my thirst here, but not in Hell
- ➤ The gospel is preached here, but not in Hell

A Christ-less Hell is the most valid expression ever given because of the irretrievable soul in Hell. Jesus is considered to be the bridge, the only way, and nobody comes to the Father but by him. (John 14:6)

God is everywhere, according to the Psalmist in Psalm 139:8; *"If I ascend up into heaven, thou art there: If I make my bed in hell, behold, thou art there."* This tells us of God's omnipresence but this does not include his passage to where God is. The day of judgment will determine our location of eternal existence, and our earthly decisions will determine our position with God by our belief in his Son. *"For God sent not his Son into the world to condemn the world; but that the world through him might be saved. He that believeth on him is not condemned: but he that believeth not is condemned already, because he hath not believed in the name of the only begotten Son of God."(John 3:17-18)*

Going back to our two verses, Romans 6:23 and Hebrews 9:27 with John 3:16-18, we can see:
- ❖ God does not want to see eternal death for any of his creation; he loved the world so much that he sent his son here to die.
- ❖ He has provided a gift, free of charge and eternal for us.
- ❖ Judgment is sure after death, not altered in any way.

Judgments Will Come

There are two judgments in Heaven-- the "Judgment Seat of Christ," and "The Great White Throne Judgment." The Judgment seat of Christ is for those that are saved, born again Christians, *"...for we shall all stand before the judgment seat of Christ."* (Rom. 14:10) The Apostle Paul was speaking to the Christian with no uncertain terms. Then he went on to explain in detail to the Corinthian church of what to expect. *"For other foundation can no man lay than that which is laid, which is Jesus Christ. Now if any man build upon this foundation gold, silver, precious stones, wood, hay, stubble; every man's work shall be* made manifest: for the day shall declare it, because it shall be revealed by fire; and the fire shall try every man's work of what sort it is. If any man's work abide which he hath built thereupon, he shall receive a reward. If any man's work shall be burned, he shall suffer loss: but he himself shall be saved; yet so as by fire." (I Cor. 3:11-15)

After the rapture, (I Thess. 4:16-17), the Christian will stand before Christ to receive a reward at his throne. The Greek word, "bema," *"Heaven is my throne, and earth is my footstool... (Acts 7:49)* is our judgment, with no condemnation, but for all we have served, by the Spirit in Christ, for the kingdom in our earthly life will now be rewarded here. All those that are written in the Lamb's Book of Life will be the only ones at this judgment. Later, in Revelation 21:27, the Bible excludes anyone else from entering into Heaven. In fact, this verse 27 states, *"And there shall in no wise enter into it any thing that defileth, neither whatsoever worketh abomination, or maketh a lie: but they which are written in the Lamb's book of life."*

A similar passage is found in Galatians 5:19-21, which lists all the works of the flesh. According to verse 21; *"....they which do such things shall not inherit the kingdom of God."* This is a threshold passage which distinguishes the unsaved from the saved. Verses 22-24 describe the spiritual; *"But the fruit of the Spirit is love, joy, peace, longsuffering, gentleness, goodness, faith, meekness, temperance: against such there is no law. And they that are Christ's have crucified the flesh with the affections and lusts."* These are those who take part in the first resurrection and judgment.

"And I saw a great white throne, and him that sat on it, from whose face the earth and the heaven fled away; and there was found no place for them. And I saw the dead, small and great, stand before God; and the books were

opened: and another book was opened, which is the book of life: and the dead were judged out of those things which were written in the books, according to their works. And the sea gave up the dead which were in it; and death and hell delivered up the dead which were in them: and they were judged every man according to their works. And death and hell were cast into the lake of fire. This is the second death. And whosoever was not found written in the book of life was cast into the lake of fire." (Rev. 20:11-15) The Bible is crystal clear here that these judged are not saved and they are categorized right along with the eternal dead that never see life because God has pronounced their judgment and that is final. The lake of fire is now the eternal destination for those who have never accepted Christ, those that end up at this judgment.

Jesus Christ will be the judge at both of these throne judgments. We can see the indication that clarifies this statement in chapter 21 of Revelation verses 5-6; *"And he that sat upon the throne said, Behold I make all things new. And he said unto me. Write: for these words are true and faithful. And he said unto me, It is done. I am Alpha and Omega, the beginning and the end. I will give unto him that is athirst of the fountain of the water of life freely."* Jesus Christ, the one that died on the cross, buried, and rose again from the dead, has victory over death and Hell and is now the judge of the entire world. He has the final say in every matter of judgment and our eternal life in Heaven.

"And there shall be no more curse: but the throne of God and of the Lamb shall be in it; and his servants shall serve him." (Rev. 22:3) Eternity in Heaven is sure, and living with our Savior throughout eternity is the best reward anyone could receive. It is our due diligence to share the good news of this Heavenly place. *"And the Spirit and the bride*

say, Come. And let him that heareth say, Come. And let him that is athirst come. And whosoever will, let him take the water of life freely." (Rev. 22:17) "He which testifieth these things saith, Surely I come quickly. Amen. Even so, come, Lord Jesus." (Rev. 22:20)

Chapter Seven

Go Ye Therefore

We find in the book of Joshua, God's direct commission to Joshua after the death of Moses; *"Moses my servant is dead; now therefore arise, go over this Jordan, thou, and all this people, unto the land which I do give to them, even to the children of Israel. Every place that the sole of your foot shall tread upon, that have I given unto you, as I said unto Moses." (Josh. 1:2-3)* It is amazing the parallel of this passage from Almighty God and the Great Commission from Jesus. Direct, demanding, with promise, and the presence of God's power to encourage the victory sure. Notice verse 9 also-- *"Have I not commanded thee? Be strong and of a good courage; be not afraid, neither be thou dismayed: for the Lord thy God is with thee withersoever thou goest."*

"Although I have shared Christ personally with many thousands of people through the years, I am rather a reserve person and do not always find it easy to witness. But, I have made this my practice, and I urge you to do the same: Assume that whenever you are alone with another person for more than a few moments, you are there by divine appointment to explain to that person the love and forgiveness he can know through faith in Jesus Christ." [7]
(Bill Bright)

[7] Bill Bright, "How To Tell Others About Christ." **Worldwide Challenge, April 1993, 17, Robert J. Morgan, Nelson's Complete Book of Stories, Illustrations, & Quotes, pg. 779**

We are sure that God wants us to march upon this earth with his Word, spreading the Gospel, sharing the hope for mankind, to every living soul. So first of all, let us examine these words starting with "courage," "amats" in the Hebrew, which means to be alert, steadfast minded, and strong. I think this means more than being brave. Peter records this type of statement in I Peter 5:8; "Be sober, be vigilant; because your adversary the devil, as a roaring lion, walketh about, seeking whom he may devour." Any good leader can mount up soldiers with a courageous intention of fighting; but this fight is with an adversary that doesn't fight fair. There are no rules or limitations, he doesn't stop at the physical, he tries to destroy your will. *"The thief cometh not, but for to steal, and to kill, and to destroy..." (John 10:10)*

Spiritual Courage

The adversary is not threatened unless your weapons are spiritual. If he can catch you unaware, unprepared, and weak in areas, that is when he will attack. For example, if you want to prepare your mind, thoughts, and commitment to God's Word, he will make it hard for you to study and make you question areas that God has made clear. All of this is an attempt to keep you from engaging in battle. What kind of soldier is unfaithful, doubting, even unbelieving at times? *"...be ye transformed by the renewing of your mind, that ye may prove what is that good, and acceptable, and perfect, will of God." (Rom.12:2)*

Courage has to be ready to take on the wiles of the enemy with a committed resolve and a plan. No great general ever went into battle and claimed victory without a great plan. You can't get lucky – because the enemy is prepared.

The enemy comes in disguise of power, fame, and fortune with all the temptations bombarding you to make you redirect your strategy or just distract you into serving yourself, not God. You can easily forget the purpose for being in battle when you are compromised. "Love not the world, neither the things that are in the world. If any man love the world, the love of the Father is not in him. For all that is in the world, the lust of the flesh, and the lust of the eyes, and the pride of life, is not of the Father, but is of the world." (I John 2:15-16) *"A double minded man is unstable in all his ways." (James 1:8)*

Fear Not

The fear factor is real and inflated by the devil. Remember that he always wants to drive your focus away from the Lord and souls that desperately need the saving grace of God. Peter stepped out of the boat to be with Jesus and to walk on the water because Jesus said in one word, "*come.*" (Mat. 14:29)

In verse 26, here in Matthew 14, Jesus was walking on the water, and the disciples thought he was a spirit and were afraid. Jesus bid them by saying in verse 27 simply; *"Be of good cheer; it is I; be not afraid."* We have a hyper-sense of fearing the unnatural and the unknown even if God has assured us that it will be alright. Fear is nothing but:

False, **E**vidence, **A**ppearing, **R**eal - by the enemy.

People have a natural fear of only two things:

- o Loud noises- you can be relaxed and hear a loud noise and it can shake every nerve in your body.

- Falling – you can be sleeping and having a wonderful dream, and find yourself falling from some steep entity and wake up with a jolt of terror.

These again are natural, not spiritual, and by putting these two issues into perspective, the mind plays on the psyche as if you had your ego suddenly stolen. Simply, your self-pride can be shattered and caught off guard, leaving you defenseless.

We can accept natural fears, but not spiritual fears. We will have to depend on the Holy Spirit because of our depraved nature that needs reinforcement and empowerment. You can't do it alone, and the enemy knows we are merely human. *"And fear not them which kill the body, but are not able to kill the soul: but rather fear him which is able to destroy both soul and body in hell."* (Mat. 10:28)

Lift Up Thy Cross

"Then said Jesus unto his disciples, If any man will come after me, let him deny himself, and take up his cross, and follow me." (Mat. 16:24) Notice that Jesus did not refer to the cross as his own, but "his," or our cross to bear. Yes, Christians do lift up the cross if you are obeying what Jesus said here, to deny yourself. The more that it is all about you, the lower that cross is lifted. When it is all about Jesus, then we lift and proclaim the book, blood, and the blessed hope with a victorious cheer.

The devil hates to see anyone lifting up the cross because his whole intention is to keep you, in any way possible, from ever gaining any attention by proclaiming the Gospel. Keeping the cross lowered and hoping nobody knows that you are a Christian makes the enemy rejoice.

The message of the cross is the most powerful message ever heard in the entire world. What other message has eternal rewards, a sacrificial foundation, a soul-changing purpose, a love motivated power, and a timeless endurance? Jesus came, Jesus died on the cross, Jesus rose again eternally, and offers eternal life, is the whole message. But, let's take a closer look at why the enemy is so offended with this glory story.

Victory Belongs to Whom?

First of all, Satan claimed a victory in the garden with Adam and Eve unleashing sin into the world. He realized that mankind could be swayed if given the right circumstances, and could then pass off to them all the sinful and devilish standards that he possesses. The immorality fashioned to fit the desires of the flesh, pleasing to the point of defending this way of life. We truly can categorize this way of life as of the Anti-Christ, totally opposite of the spiritual values of God. This created an everlasting world of blind followers without spiritual substance and no reason to change.

We can see how the line has been drawn to be on one side or the other. Jesus saw and warned of this division; *"He that is not with me is against me: and he that gathereth not with me scattereth." (Luke 11:23)*

For example, in I Samuel 17, King Saul and all the armies of Israel occupied one side of the valley of Elah, while across the way stood the Philistine army with this arrogant giant, like an attack dog, protecting their side. Both armies are on the mountain tops listening to Goliath carry on about how he defied Israel and cannot be defeated. We know how the story ends, when we find a courageous young man, filled with godly indignation, proceeding across the valley with nothing but a sling and the Spirit of God upon him, victoriously slaying the impenetrable force. The enemy is nothing without followers to support his agenda, but they are nothing in the face of Almighty God.

In Revelation 20:7-10 we read; *"And when the thousand years are expired, Satan shall be loosed out of his prison, and shall go out to deceive the nations which are in the four quarters of the earth, Gog and Magog, to gather them together to battle: the number of whom is as the sand of the sea. And they went up on the breadth of the earth, and compassed the camp of the saints about, and the beloved city: and fire came down from God out of heaven, and devoured them. And the devil that deceived them was cast into the lake of fire and brimstone, where the beast and the false prophet are, and shall be tormented day and night for ever and ever."* This is the nature of Satan, to never give up destroying the lives of people with help from other people. This pretty much describes our ungodly society today, tragically and inevitably going this direction. *"There is a way which seemeth right unto a man, but the end thereof are the ways of death." (Prov. 14:12)* Almighty God will not let him succeed regardless of his stubborn efforts.

Secondly, he offers promises to people that appeal to the flesh with no spiritual value. In Matthew 4:1-11, we see the incident when Satan tried to tempt Jesus. He found Jesus fasting in a supposed weakened condition of hunger and stated; *"If thou be the Son of God, command that these stones be made bread."* Food for the body? Yes, that has temporal value for all humanity, but nothing for the soul. You see, Satan has no divinity, but he pretends to while he offers mankind a pleasing deal. The world and all that is in it belongs to God, but he has persuaded the world that he owns everything and that he needs to come to him to get it. We don't need a middle man that offers us the Brooklyn

Bridge. Jesus' reply to the failed attempt was, *"It is written, Man shall not live by bread alone, but by every word that proceedeth out of the mouth of God."*

Satan continues to offer Jesus fame, fortune, and the kingdoms of this world if he would just fall down and worship him. Again Jesus replies, *"Get thee hence Satan: for it is written, Thou shalt worship the Lord thy God, and him only shalt thou serve."*

We should agree that Satan uses man's pride to manipulate him to serve him and self. And we know how God feels about pride; *"Pride goeth before destruction, and an haughty spirit before a fall." (Prov. 16:18)* Pride tends to inflate man's worst behavior.

"For all that is in the world, the lust of the flesh, and the lust of the eyes, and the pride of life, is not of the Father, but is of the world. And the world passeth away, and the lust thereof: but he that doeth the will of God abideth for ever." (I John 2:16-17) The road to serving God is well-traveled and leads to eternal success, as the road to serving the enemy is well entreating and leads to a waste of time and effort. Distraction for the soul-winner needs to remain part of the scenery, not a destination.

Obedience is the only course for victory. Focus on God's purpose, for our duty is at hand and achievable. *"For though we walk in the flesh, we do not war after the flesh: (For the weapons of our warfare are not carnal, but mighty through God to the pulling down of strong holds;) Casting down imaginations, and every high thing that exalteth itself against the knowledge of God, and bringing into captivity every thought to the obedience of Christ; and having in a readiness to revenge all disobedience, when your obedience is fulfilled." (II Cor. 10:3-6)*

Go ye therefore because the world needs you to lift up that cross, tell the truth, and open the eyes of the blind to accept the forgiveness of Christ unto life eternal. *"But the anointing which ye have received of him abideth in you, and ye need not that any man teach you: but as the same anointing teacheth you of all things, and is truth, and is no lie, and even as it hath taught you, ye shall abide in him." (I John 2:27)* Less than one percent of Christians today are engaged in evangelism. Should we turn a deaf ear to the voice of God, or is it that we are not trusting that God can use us for His perfect will? The road easiest traveled is the road the world takes daily, but most know that their life is empty of any spiritual satisfaction.

"There is no fear in love; but perfect love casteth out fear." I John 4:18

Chapter Eight

Many are Called, Few are Chosen

Would you take the same wage for doing eleven hours of work that a person was paid for one hour of work? We would cry unfair, maybe get the union involved, go to human resources, or call a strike. Jesus told a parable of the labourers in Matthew 20 that confronts this issue. Surprising enough, the lord of the vineyard paid everyone the same wage for coming to work on the first hour as the eleventh hour.

The verses that really sum up this passage are verses 15 and 16 where Jesus states, *"Is it not lawful for me to do what I will with mine own? Is thine eye evil, because I am good? So the last shall be first, and the first last: for many be called, but few chosen."*

The Life Plan

Nobody can instruct God on his selective service because he can see the outcome. Things in this life don't always go as planned, therefore a random domino effect happens more than we know. In other words, the perfect plan of God in each individual's life rarely gets fulfilled. God can see where things of our lives and the world have gone awry to a certain extent, so he continually shares wisdom to keep his sovereign plan on course.

So the mystery presents itself of why God chooses certain people to do a specific duty when others just as important could do it. Many can't see the big picture because their individual need comes first. The Apostle Paul had wisdom concerning this mystery in I Corinthians 1:26-29; *"For ye see your calling, brethren, how that not many wise men after the flesh, not many mighty, not many noble, are called: But God hath chosen the foolish things of the world to confound the wise; and God hath chosen the weak things of the world to confound the things which are mighty; And base things of the world, and things which are despised, hath God chosen, yea, and things which are not, to bring to nought things that are: That no flesh should glory in his presence."* Well-known biblical examples such as Noah, Enoch, Abraham, Elijah, Daniel, David, Gideon, and Paul, have manifested such spiritual feats of faith; and the mystery remains today, even to the end of this age of grace.

Jacob blessed his sons before he died and it kind of seems strange that he could prophesy their lives and their descendants. God gave him this insight to pronounce their purpose on this earth. Others as Jonah would be selected to carry out God's orders while totally defiant against God. Jonah knew the mercy of God, that he would give Nineveh a chance to repent. Jonah knew the big picture and fled.

Saul of Tarsus was a man dangerous to be around, armed with biblical knowledge and a great zeal for setting the world straight. Jesus knew that this man's zeal was misdirected and damaging to the grace of God and the purpose for which Jesus died on the cross. Acts 9:1 characterizes Saul's attitude as *"...yet breathing out threatenings and slaughter against the disciples of the Lord."*

Why should the Lord choose people like this for such an important purpose when they seem to be uncooperative? It all has to do with His divine plan and what he knows about the potential of these individuals. Paul called himself the "chief of sinners" after Salvation as Jesus knew he would. Therefore, he went from persecutor to humble servant whose eyes were opened to the truth and opportunity of the cross to change eternity. There will be individuals who will meet the challenge of soul-winning whose souls have been miraculously saved, and they can see clearly what the enemy is doing and feel obligated (called) to be steadfast in the advances of the cross to lead as many people to Christ as possible. God has given them a spirit-filled drive.

David declared in Psalm 8:3-5; *"When I consider thy heavens, the work of thy fingers, the moon and the stars, which thou hast ordained; What is man, that thou art mindful of him? and the son of man, that thou visitest him? For thou hast made him a little lower than the angels, and hast crowned him with glory and honour."* David saw the big picture, God's plan for the world, he was Heavenly minded and a man after God's own heart, but still sinned against God. But through all of David's backsliding, God knew this man's heart. He was a prime example of choosing the wrong authority on occasion.(see chapter 3 of this book) The time he sinned in the flesh, was the time his soul made the wrong decision to follow the wrong authority. Nonetheless, God's grace comes and shows us our failures and the spirit-filled, spirit-led, servant will get back on track, see the big picture, and have an uncanny way of growing from their experience and their drive is unstoppable. *"This I say then, Walk in the Spirit, and ye shall not fulfil the lust of the flesh." (Gal. 5:16)*

This refining character of the Holy Spirit is the one thing every Christian relies on to help them grow. He will purify our souls and cleanse us from all unrighteousness. (I John 1:9) God sees and knows all our infirmities and chooses to use us anyway.

God's Choice, Our Commitment to Evangelize

The question today is, why does God choose one over the other in evangelism? The answer comes in the form of renewing. How does the Olympian become the best in their field? It is more than practice and repetition. I have seen many witnesses for Christ that are faithful in going out with the church and passing out tracts, but the fruit of their labors are lean. The cunning action of the enemy has engaged on these that do the same thing every time. You have to try to out- smart the devil. *"Behold, I send you forth as sheep in the midst of wolves: be ye therefore wise as serpents, and harmless as doves." (Mat. 10:16)*

Don't get me wrong, everyone is called to be a part of the "Great Commission" and witness, but there will be some that excel because of their commitment of never giving up and constantly renewing their craftiness. Jonathan Edwards gave us a bold resolution;

"Resolved, to improve every opportunity, when I am in the best and happiest frame of mind, to cast and venture my soul on the Lord Jesus Christ, to trust and confide in him, and consecrate myself wholly to him; that from this I may have assurance of my safety, knowing that I confide in my Redeemer." (July 8, 1723)

"And be not conformed to this world: but be ye transformed by the renewing of your mind, that ye may prove what is that good, and acceptable, and perfect, will of God." (Rom. 12:2) Being transformed from this world is not the focus here as much as the renewing of the mind, which is our soul's main agent, to prove and improve your obligation to God's will. I will be as bold as to say, that if you are victorious in rescuing lost souls from the enemy in a dying, cursed, Hell-driven world in which we live, you are undeniably fulfilling God's Perfect Will!

You will find that there are three different levels of people willing to evangelize:

- ➢ Level One – The witness that will share their faith and invite people to church.
- ➢ Level Two – The soul-winner who will share their faith and are determined to lead someone to Christ.
- ➢ Level Three – The soul-winner who is determined to lead people to Christ; who are fearless, fire-breathing, spirit-led individuals, who want to impact the world for Christ. The souls of people have become their life-long burden.

Soul Warrior

Let's look at the level three soul-winner to understand how someone could become such a "Soul Warrior" for Christ. In Hebrews 11; the whole chapter is dedicated to those courageous individuals who offered up their lives to be faithful to God.

"And others had trial of cruel mockings and scourgings, yea, moreover of bonds and imprisonment: they were stoned, they were sawn asunder, were tempted, were slain with the sword: they wandered about in sheepskins and goatskins; being destitute, afflicted, tormented; (of whom the world was not worthy:) they wandered in deserts, and in mountains, and in dens and caves of the earth. And these all, having obtained a good report through faith, received not the promise: God having provided some better thing for us, that they without us should not be made perfect." (Heb. 11:36-40) This kind of person served God and never saw earthly rewards, but followed God for the Heavenly rewards. Missionaries would fall into this category in many ways because of their unstoppable drive to change the world for Jesus Christ. The Soul Warrior is such an individual that is needed in our churches and society today. The church needs someone willing to take

the lead in church evangelism; going outside the church to win souls and increase the church, which will impact the community.

Evangelism has been neglected too long in many churches, resulting in no new life lifting the very souls of our pastors and members to see the miraculous work of God, to give everyone a fresh purpose and stronger faith. We wonder why people are not as committed in church attendance and involvement as the old days. Boring and irrelevant are the latest comments from the folks you ask today about church attendance. People need to see fire from Heaven, so to say, to be a part of the victory over the enemy and to see God moving.

Staff Evangelists Needed

Every single New Testament Church today needs a Staff Evangelist to lead and to teach people to be soul-winners, so the church can stand strong in the Lord and on the foundation on which Jesus died on the cross to give Salvation to the world, starting with your local church. *"...the gates of hell shall not prevail against it." (Mat. 16:18)* Advancement of the church is ordained by the Lord, unstoppable, and commissioned to win souls. This is not the duty of the Pastor, who equips the Saints and oversees the church and all activities thereof. (more mention later in chapter 9) If your church does not have a staff evangelist, a person that would be considered a Soul Warrior armed with the whole armor of God, prayer is much needed. God will provide your church with such an individual if he sees the genuine burden for lost souls in your church. Remember that God never asks us to do something that he doesn't provide.

It is a good possibility that a Soul Warrior is in a great Bible-believing church, but the church is turning its focus away from lost souls and is replacing it with sensational worship and new programs, all the while starting to ignore the "Great Commission." You as a Soul Warrior will need to find a church where God wants you to relocate if you can't persuade them of the importance of Salvation that they are so recklessly leaving behind.

Paul's charge to Timothy applies to all evangelists; *"For the time will come when they will not endure sound doctrine; but after their own lusts shall they heap to themselves teachers, having itching ears; and they shall turn away their ears from the truth, and shall be turned unto fables. But watch thou in all things, endure afflictions, do the work of an evangelist, make full proof of thy ministry." (II Tim. 4:3-5)*

Many are called, but there are only a few that will take this call as priority because of the love they have for people and the noticeable decline they see of souls being saved.

It is not enough to go with the crowd on these matters. Someone has to take the mantle and stand in the stream of an ever-flowing culture of unbelief and moral corruption. *"Looking for that blessed hope, and the glorious appearing of the great God and our Savior Jesus Christ." (Titus 2:13)*

"Those whom God has chosen are led by the Holy Spirit to choose God and his way of salvation ….the chosen of the Lord are led to relinquish the proud way of self and merit: they take to the road of faith, and so find rest unto their souls." (C.H. Spurgeon)

Chapter Nine

The Soul Patrol

Can a person ever be overworked, overscheduled, loaded with responsibilities to the point of resignation? It's funny how an employee can quit a job and it takes three employees to do the work that they were doing alone. No wonder they quit. You can gradually accumulate more than you can bear if you are not aware of it. Psychologists make a good living by helping people that are at their breaking point. You might be strong and have a great endurance, while others are seeing the toll that it is taking on you.

Spirit is Willing, the Flesh is Weak

In the book of Exodus chapter 18, starting in verse 13; "And it came to pass on the morrow, that Moses sat to judge the people: and the people stood by Moses from the morning unto the evening. And when Moses' father in law saw all that he did to the people, he said, What is this thing thou doest to the people? why sittest thou thyself alone, and all the people stand by thee from morning unto even? And Moses said unto his father in law, Because the people come unto me to enquire of God: When they have a matter, they come unto me; and I judge between one and another, and I do make them know the statutes of God, and his laws. And Moses' father in law said unto him, The thing that thou doest is not good. Thou wilt surely wear away, both thou, and this people that is with thee: for this thing is too heavy for thee: thou are not able to perform it *thyself alone."* Burn-out was in Moses' future if he continued serving God at this capacity.

There is no denying that God called Moses to lead this great mass of over two million people over a vast land to freedom. Moses had his heart in the right place. The people needed counsel, but why take this on alone? No doubt this counsel started with one or two disputes, then six or eight, ten or twelve, etc., and accumulated into an exasperating duty that nobody could draw an ounce of joy from. It is difficult to serve God without some level of joy and accomplishment.

Churches are guilty of putting a willing, warm body in a position that they don't belong in or have a spiritual gift for, with a result of burn-out. The same thing was happening to Moses. He was commanded by God to deliver the children of Israel out of Egyptian bondage, but was he commanded to give counsel to a relentless people that drained him of his wisdom and time?

We must be careful of taking on too much and other responsibilities than what the true and original calling entails. The enemy would love to see our duty distracted and side-tracked to the point of a half-hearted effort of serving God. Remember the verse in James 1:8; *"A double minded man is unstable in all his ways."* Meaning, the main thing has to stay the main thing.

Keeping the Call

"Moreover thou shalt provide out of all the people able men, such as fear God, men of truth, hating covetousness; and place such over them, to be rulers of thousands, and rulers of hundreds, rulers of fifties, and rulers of tens." (Ex. 18:21) This is the position of pastors, teachers, and administrators, but not the position of an evangelist. The evangelist is wise, but his wisdom deals with salvation

being the main thrust of his calling. To be as effectual in the ministry of evangelism, you must be committed to a certain discernment of foundational truth. Salvation first is always the most important level of Christianity to you.

The old saying about being fishers of men; "We catch them, God will clean them," is fine with the evangelist. Moses delivered the children of Israel, but Aaron was in the position of the priest. We can see that Moses never went into the promised land, of course, God wouldn't let him because of his disobedience, but I am not sure that he was ever meant to go in at all. *"Fear ye not, stand still, and see the salvation of the Lord." (Ex. 14:13)* was the cry of the evangelist who leads the people to the promised land. In our case, Heaven is our promised destination.

Only a committed servant like Moses could do this huge undertaking that God called him to. God knew that he could use this imperfect man to carry out the deliverance and message and purpose. This man had a heart of a courageous warrior to pick up the mantle and march on to victory. He had the heart of a lion.

So, how can a Staff Evangelist/Soul Warrior take on such a responsibility? He can't go it alone, he can't be unwise to burn-out, he has the zeal, and his calling is sure. The devil will not let his people go; the captives are under bondage and strongholds of serving the wrong master.

The challenge involves creating a group of followers that will answer the call for winning the lost for Christ. The church and the Pastor can play a very important role in this spiritual selection by giving this new leader time to teach, preach, and present the Gospel and vision to the congregation. People will get saved by much prayer, and this will be the proof that God's hand is on this ministry. Once people see this spiritual victory happening in the church, they will get curious and God will start to work on their heart to become a part of this life-changing ministry. It has been said many times that this ministry is "not taught, but caught." This means that mortal man doesn't do much of the teaching; the Holy Spirit makes you a student, and he never stops until he has opened every avenue of your heart and soul to give you wisdom and the vision to win. Don't get me wrong, there will be some instruction and planning.

This new group will start by a few being interested to know more of the strategy to win the lost. Let me remind you again that this is not the responsibility of the pastor to lead this ministry, he has his duties to care for and equip the saints already. *"And he gave some, apostles; and some, prophets; and some, evangelists; and some, pastors and teachers; For the perfecting of the saints, for the work of the ministry, for the edifying of the body of Christ." (Eph. 4:11-12)* If this ministry were to fall on the Pastor, it would be over-bearing and make him feel guilty of not putting all of his time in it. Therefore God will appoint someone to be the leader.

Organize

Organization is very important for scheduling time for the class to train and to instruct the vision of Salvation and winning the lost for Christ. The leader will have to cast a vision that never alters and never compromises. This vision is worth taking to your grave because it has been sent from on high. From Almighty God to his humble and obedient servants. Methodology must work in this commission, but the vision and message has to remain the same, age after age, generation by generation. Our message is, that God sent his Son to be born of a virgin, he lived on this earth long enough to die on a cross for our sins, he was buried and rose from the dead, he lives forever in Heaven to offer mankind forgiveness of sin, and eternal life. Jesus said, *"...Verily, verily, I say unto thee, Except a man be born again, he cannot see the kingdom of God." (John 3:3)* This is the "Good News," the Gospel of Jesus Christ!

This ministry is embarking on changing eternity and the course of history. Imagine if some of the great men of the past had never been saved, such as George Washington, Abraham Lincoln, D. L. Moody, C.H Spurgeon, Billy Graham, and many more; the world would be different today.

We will have to start with a vision, then willing messengers, with one soul won at a time, to build the ministry. Like our faith is built gradually, such is the soul-winning ministry. *"It is like a grain of mustard seed, which a man took, and cast into his garden; and it grew, and waxed a great tree; and the fowls of the air lodged in the branches of it." (Luke 13:19)* When the growth becomes evident, the interest will multiply and new life will spring up.

Territory

One thing we have to keep in mind is that the enemy will think that we are trespassing on his territory as we march on to win souls in our towns and cities. For some reason, he thinks he owns the very ground we are conquering. Paul referred to Satan as the *"prince of the power of the air"* in Ephesians 2:2, and that spirit works in the children of disobedience. Consequently, he is a prince with blinded followers, loyal to evil power and influence. A prince is usually awarded a usual section of territory, such as a country to rule over, but this prince rules over all the spiritually dead wherever they may be located in this world; which is everywhere.

Have you ever been in an airplane and noticed as you gained altitude that you could start seeing more of the city the higher you got? Then comes a point when you can see the whole city before you go above the clouds. The view looks even more spectacular at night with the lights everywhere below you. You can see the boundaries of the whole city at once. Consider that this city has been claimed by this prince and his followers. The political arena that governs that territory has had an influence of corrupted values and policies. The system is difficult to challenge to gain any ground. But, we are not called to take control of the ground, just sow the seeds and let God give the increase.

Tares

Jesus spoke of this entanglement in Matthew 13:24-26; *"The kingdom of heaven is likened unto a man which sowed good seed in his field: But while men slept, his enemy came and sowed tares among the wheat, and went his way. But when the blade was sprung up, and brought forth fruit, then appeared the tares also."* He continued in verses 28-29 to state, *"...The servants said unto him, Wilt thou then that we go and gather them up? But he said, Nay; lest while ye gather up the tares, ye root up also the wheat with them."* So this has to be accepted among the soul-winner. Make no mistake, God will separate these tares out one day and prove that this world still belongs to him, no matter how busy the enemy has been to dominate this earth.

False Religions

What are some of the tares that are obvious? The one that is most dangerous is not that man is blind, but provides some false religions. You can see a vast variety springing up everywhere. Mosques, Temples, and Shrines are becoming more accepted across the United States as well as the world. The danger is a counterfeit worship because the enemy knows that God created man with this relationship need for him, where we cry, "Abba," Father. Jesus said, *"Get thee hence, Satan: for it is written, Thou shalt worship the Lord thy God, and him only shalt thou serve." (Mat. 4:10)*

Riches

Another tare would be money and the power thereof. Paul warned us about this danger in I Timothy 6:10; *"For the love of money is the root of all evil: which while some coveted after, they have erred from the faith, and pierced themselves through with many sorrows."* This is huge among the lost and the saved alike. Lives are ruined and forever damaged by the greed and lust of more money. This root goes deep into our souls and rules men to weakness with temptations and bad decisions thereof. There seems to be a bigger and better deal offered you, but these deals keep your mind off what God wants, and puts your interests first. There are many wealthy people in the Bible, but they prayed for the wisdom of God in their lives. It is not a sin to have wealth, but our attitude about money means everything to your walk with God. *"But my God shall supply all your need according to his riches in glory by Christ Jesus." (Phil. 4:19)* God has your interest in mind, believe it or not, when this promise is accepted by you.

Soldiers On Patrol

Let's agree that the world is infiltrated with Satan's accomplishments and no man can come close to effectively stopping this advancement. We will need a group of messengers to expose the Word of God on a consistent schedule to the people to slow down these advancements so people can start having their own personal victories in Christ. In other words, plant the seeds consistently to root righteous thinking. This group must be on patrol with a strategy to saturate the community with the saving knowledge of Jesus Christ. The territory belongs to God and the fullness thereof, so we are not trespassing; we have a right of passage by God the Father and the Lord Jesus Christ when he said, *"All power is given unto me in heaven and in earth. Go ye therefore, and teach all nations, baptizing them in the name of the Father, and of the Son, and of the Holy Ghost: Teaching them to observe all things whatsoever I have commanded you."* (Mat. 28:18-20)

"We are called to be soldiers of Christ, and to bear His name in America will require greater commitment and self-sacrifice in the days ahead. If we are to reclaim lost ground, we need to avoid compromise and incessant flirting with the world. We are in a serious battle with great issues at stake." 8 *(D. James Kennedy)*

Precious souls are at stake and we have the responsibility to reach them before the enemy destroys them. Jesus said in Matthew 4:19; *"Follow me, and I will make you fishers of men."* Meaning, that the world is like a great sea of people that are dear and precious to God, and what is the best strategy to catch them? This is not a passive approach or a lifestyle type of evangelism, but an aggressive, planned out approach with a leader who knows where the fish are.

People move around continuously; new neighborhoods, new relatives, new homes being built, newly- weds--ever changing and hard to keep track of it all. The Lord sees it all and can point out any different activity that we should notice. As the policemen patrol their assigned areas, they notice anything different-- cars, homes, disturbances, etc.

8 D. James Kennedy, The Gates of Hell Shall Not Prevail, Thomas Nelson Publishers, pg. 216

The soul-winner should be aggressive to the point of going on patrol to be continuously aware of any opportunity that arises. If there is anything different about a neighborhood, the New Soul Patrol should be present and curious that somebody might have moved in and needs Salvation. Every church would be wise to have a Soul Patrol, to be familiar with any new prospects that need saved, baptized, taught, and become new members of the church.

The Soul Patrol taught by the Soul Warrior/Staff Evangelist should always meet in discussion of the current plan to cover prayerfully the area directed by the Lord. Dividing into areas two by two would be the idea as Jesus sent out his disciples.

Some are well-advanced in social media and communications, which is a very popular area of interest and opportunity to reach people. You don't have to try to mislead anyone down a rabbit hole, then trap them, because people will start to be aware to avoid certain sites that would practice this. Be clear and concise to present the Gospel boldly. There are people out there that will respond because God is already working on their hearts. Keep this in mind every time you go out to share the Gospel, that the field is ripe for harvest, like Jesus said. It is amazing how the enemy tries to make you give up right before you reach the one that gets saved. Be wise to listen to the leader on these issues. The more you engage in soul-winning, the wiser you become.

Essentials

Here are some Essentials for the Soul-Winner and the Soul Patrol to keep in mind:

- ❖ People are lost and we know the way – Mat. 9:36-38
    - o They have no shepherd – (Vs. 36)

- - Who will care as Jesus does – (Vs. 36)
  - Your challenge is clear – (Vs. 37)
  - The Harvest belongs to Jesus – (Vs. 38)
- ❖ Our humility is needed every time. – James 4:10
  - Jesus had humility before the Father – (Luke 22:42)
  - Paul's humility to become all things to all men – (I Cor. 9:22)
  - Weakness will become strength – (II Cor. 12:10)
- ❖ Obedience is required – Isa. 6:8-10
  - Nobody gets saved without going – (Rom. 10:17)
  - The Holy Spirit helps you yield – (II Cor. 1:22, Rom. 6:19)
- ❖ Go believing – Rom. 1:16, Psa. 126:6

Every time we lead someone to the Lord, we will experience a heavenly joy beyond compare. The Lord will touch you deeply with a spiritual sense of feeling the love as he does. Then our spiritual growth leaps in all areas because of our desire to be close and our walk with God deepens. Our Greatest Opportunity becomes a whole-hearted commitment and dedication to Almighty God. Win the Victory!

Chapter Ten

The Lordship of Jesus Christ

The old saying goes like this; *"If he is not Lord of all, he is not Lord at all."* Wait a minute. I go to church and I think of what Jesus would do in every situation so I can emulate him. Isn't that enough?

The Bible says in Philippians 2:9-13; *"Wherefore God also hath highly exalted him, and given him a name which is above every name: That at the name of Jesus every knee should bow, of things in heaven, and things in earth, and things under the earth; And that every tongue should confess that Jesus Christ is Lord, to the glory of God the Father. Wherefore, my beloved, as ye have always obeyed, not as in my presence only, but now much more in my absence, work out your own salvation with fear and trembling. For it is God which worketh in you both to will and to do of his good pleasure."*

Jesus is the bride groom of the church, and all churches conduct differently, but what does that have to do with you? You don't serve the church, you serve God through Christ.

The church is the vehicle and platform for reaching the lost world, and if your church is not attempting to do the will of God, that church is in disobedience to His Will. You on the other hand, have the Holy Spirit in you to no limit. You can walk away from a church service and feel that you have not filled any purpose or have satisfied the need for personal wisdom. All I am saying is that it is not necessary to change worship methods in a church, it is time to change you into someone beyond limitations of the church walls. *"You were made for a mission. God is at work in the world, and he wants you to join him. The assignment is called your mission. God wants you to have both a mission in the Body of Christ and a mission in the world."* 9 *(Rick Warren)*

Deity

Jesus has all power in Heaven and earth, so how far can he go to penetration of the heart, soul, and mind? Earthly elements could not limit Jesus when he walked as a man. Walking on water, controlling the weather, and food and water distributions were merely signs of an omnipotent Lord Jesus Christ. Nature bowed at his Divine Presence.

Let us focus on what we cannot understand in our finite minds for a while. He has power over demons; *"And Jesus rebuked him, saying, Hold thy peace, and come out of him. And when the devil had thrown him in the midst, he came out of him, and hurt him not." (Luke 4:35)* Jesus has power over death, Hell, and the resurrection; *"I am he that liveth, and was dead; and, behold, I am alive for evermore, Amen; and have the keys of hell and of death." (Rev. 1:18) "For as in Adam all die, even so in Christ shall all be made alive." (I Cor. 15:22)* What sort of power can this be?

When I was a child, I thought as a child, or as the Bible says, *"I spake as a child, I understood as a child."* We do see through a "glass darkly," because we seem to forget that this Holy, Divine Spirit has been passed onto us to do the work Jesus gave his life for. It can't be acceptable to go

9 Rick Warren, *The Purpose Driven Life*, Zondervan, pg. 281

to our weekly recharge and maintain a low level of spirituality that gives us a buzz and shows a dim light of purpose. Ask yourself, "what think ye of Christ?" We owe our eternal living soul to him, and it is time to clearly visualize the Heavenly Jesus with our faith and intimacy.

The Lord Jesus Christ has dominion over Heaven and earth, and believe it or not, you are a big part of the equation. The power that is in you is greater than he that is in the world, as *I John 4:4 states,* but being a part means to let Jesus and the Holy Spirit penetrate your heart and mind to the point of visualizing the lost world from his point of view; *"For the earth is the Lord's, and the fulness thereof." (I Cor. 10:26)*

The Enemy's Deception

When Satan was banned into his second heavenly realm, he became the single most deterrent of mankind to accept Christ. What does he have to offer? Worldly wealth, fame, and influence seem to be his most obvious weapons of warfare. People march to these in a most astonishing rate and don't see what the enemy of the soul is up to. *"For we wrestle not against flesh and blood, but against principalities, against powers, against the rulers of the darkness of this world, against spiritual wickedness in high places." (Eph. 6:12)*

The insight to knowing the wiles of this devil has truly been placed in your psyche because you were once lost. All you have to do is meditate on the very things and ways that had influence over you. Ask yourself, why do I still have thoughts that draw me into certain ungodly scenarios? What is the true meaning of overcoming? Jesus said in John 16:33; *"...I have overcome the world."*

But for you and I, we have to start by not allowing our sins, weaknesses, and attachments to lead us.

Our Charter and Commission

Take a close look at our Charter or our Personal Commission, found in Eph. 1:4-5; ***"According as he hath chosen us in him before the foundation of the world, that we should be holy and without blame before him in love: Having predestinated us unto the adoption of children by Jesus Christ to himself, according to the good pleasure of his will."*** This means that Jesus had planned before the world began to use us to do His Will. What is His Will? To change people's lives. This starts at Salvation, and he continues to change us to make more disciples and to win more souls. The cycle never stops unless we ourselves try to work against it in not obeying his orders. *"That we should be holy,"* kind of stands out in our commission, because it means to be separate. This goes back to leaving all worldliness behind and focusing directly on his divine purpose.

Our Field is a Fallen World

So let's consider the facts. We live in a cursed and fallen world, which means that we exist in a realm of non-spiritual and ungodly territory that seems as dense as gravity itself, pulling at every living soul. Mankind has a free will to live and decide for themselves, to follow Jesus or any other religion set up by the enemy to keep man sinful and short of the glory of God. We have people that accept and go to church, worship God, and keep the soul clean and prayed up; and lastly, we have servants that can't accept engaging in soul warfare, but stay safely behind the trenches and front lines.

The enemy does not keep a safe distance from you, but we practice living in the deception that somehow we are keeping in a safe boundary line from him. This boundary is non-existent; he is so subtle that he creeps in unaware. *"But be ye doers of the word, and not hearers only, deceiving your own selves. For if any be a hearer of the word, and not a doer, he is like unto a man beholding his natural face in a glass: For he beholdeth himself, and goeth his way, and straightway forgetteth what manner of man he was." (James 1:22-24)*

Jesus is the Owner

People on planet earth need to wake up to the fact that Jesus owns it all, the devil thinks he owns it all, and the battle is raging. Either you are fighting (pushing forward), or you are in alliance with most of the world and slipping back, continuously fighting for air to stay alive. The question has to be asked; how long do you intend to stay lukewarm? *"Because thou sayest, I am rich, and increased with goods, and have need of nothing; and knowest not that thou are wretched, and miserable, and poor, and blind, and naked." (Rev. 3:17)* Can a Pastor say these things to a congregation and not drive people away? *"He that hath an ear, let him hear what the Spirit saith unto the churches." (Rev. 3:22)* Does this apply for today or just to the seven churches of Revelation? Does Jesus have the authority to judge my church? And will churches come up short for reaching people for Christ? All good and the right questions to meditate on before judgement. *"Why do the heathen rage, and the people imagine a vain thing? The kings of the earth set themselves, and the rulers take counsel together, against the Lord, and against his anointed, saying, Let us break their bands asunder, and cast away their cords from us. He that sitteth in the heavens shall laugh: the Lord shall have them in derision. Then shall he speak unto them in his wrath, and vex them in his sore displeasure. Yet have I set my king upon my holy hill of Zion. I will declare the decree: the Lord hath said unto me, Thou art my Son; this day have I begotten thee. Ask of me, and I shall give thee the heathen for thine inheritance, and the uttermost parts of the earth for thy possession."(Psa. 2:1-8)*

Truth and Authority

"I am the way, the truth, and the life: no man cometh unto the Father, but by me." (John 14:6) The only one who can claim this position is the Lord Jesus Christ. If you believe that he is the "way" into Heaven and true spirituality, and you believe he is the "truth," not a false picture of hope, and the "life" eternal that starts at conversion, then you share the God-ordained, solid platform of power and victory.

"People say, 'I want to know what is the truth?' Listen: 'I AM THE TRUTH,' says Christ. If you want to know what the truth is, get acquainted with Christ. People also complain that they have not life. Many are trying to give themselves spiritual life. You may galvanize yourselves and put electricity into yourselves, so to speak; but the effect will not last very long. Christ alone is the author of life. If you would have real spiritual life, get to know Christ. Many try to stir up spiritual life by going to meetings. That may be well enough, but it will be of no use, unless they get into contact with the living Christ. Then their spiritual life will not be a spasmodic thing, but will be perpetual; flowing on and on, and bringing forth the fruit to God." (D. L. Moody)

If God be for us, who can stand against us? That is what true Authority looks like-- knowing, never doubting, if we live or die, we are the Lord's. He is The Authority! *"And being made perfect, he became the author of eternal salvation unto all them that obey him." (Heb. 5:9)*

"And there shall come forth a rod out of the stem of Jesse, and a Branch shall grow out of his roots: And the Spirit of the Lord shall rest upon him, the spirit of wisdom and understanding, the spirit of counsel and might, the spirit of knowledge and of the fear of the Lord; And shall make him of quick understanding in the fear of the Lord: and he shall not judge after the sight of eyes, neither reprove after the hearing of his ears: But with righteousness shall he judge the poor, and reprove with equity for the meek of the earth: and he shall smite the earth with the rod of his mouth, and with the breath of his lips shall he slay the wicked." (Isa. 11:1-4) Jesus is the one who will be standing in the clouds of glory removing his Christians out of the earthly realm before the great tribulation, and he is also the one that leads the charge with ten thousands of his saints at Armageddon, and sets up his millennial kingdom, and he is the Lord who we will serve for all of eternity.

Jesus is preeminent, the Alpha and Omega, he was there when God the Father brought our world into existence, and he will have the last say and judgment when it comes to the entire history of this world; the times and all souls are in his hands.

In Reverence

Jesus is the only one who stretched out his arms in love, and they nailed him to a cruel cross. His blood and his body became our sin offering. We can't put the blame on the regime of the day, when all they prophetically did was to be used as an instrument to accomplish what God the Father intended to do, with the will of his only begotten Son all along. It was the sin of all mankind that kept him on that cross; he came to die that we may have life!

If we investigate the sacramental influences that each New Testament church practices; we can see that the symbols of his body, the bread, and his blood, the wine, are more for the benefits of the soul than just a memorial service. *"Verily, verily, I say unto you, Except ye eat the flesh of the Son of man, and drink his blood, ye have no life in you. Whoso eateth my flesh, and drinketh my blood, hath eternal life; and I will raise him up at the last day. For my flesh is meat indeed, and my blood is drink indeed. He that eateth my flesh, and drinketh my blood, dwelleth in me, and I in him. As the living Father hath sent me, and I live by the Father: so he that eateth me, even he shall live by me. This is that bread which came down from heaven: not as your fathers did eat manna, and are dead: he that eateth of this bread shall live for ever." (John 6:53-58)*

When we partake of the Lord's Supper or Sacramental Service, we are overlooking the fact that the symbolization is meant for the perpetual significance to eternal life. In other words, the funeral service that we all have experienced in these services, in reality, is a charge to the saints. Communion is the same as the communication to pass along the Salvation charge to the partaker. More like a solemn celebration to keep in mind that Jesus gave up himself as a sacrifice for all. This service does not save you, but it represents the power of the one who can. The Father communicates to the Son, and the Son communicates to his disciples. Immortality is at hand by the Father through the Son onto the believer.

"This do in remembrance of me..." (Luke 22, I Cor. 11), is the propagation of the Salvation message, just as God telling Adam and Eve to *"Be fruitful, and multiply, and replenish the earth, and subdue it..." (Gen. 1:28)* Remember Jesus telling his disciples that all power in Heaven and earth has been given him. He has blessed us to fulfill His Will and to reach every person on earth with the glorious Gospel of "life eternal." *"For as often as ye eat this bread, and drink this cup, ye do shew the Lord's death till he come." (I Cor. 11:26)*

Hear His Voice

"To the general assembly and church of the firstborn, which are written in heaven, and to God the Judge of all, and to the spirits of just men made perfect, And to Jesus the mediator of the new covenant, and to the blood of sprinkling, that speaketh better things that of Abel. See that ye refuse not him that speaketh. For if they escaped not who refused him that spake on earth, much more shall not we escape, if we turn away from him that speaketh from heaven: Whose voice then shook the earth: but now he hath promised, saying, Yet once more I shake not the earth only, but also heaven. And this word, yet once more, signifieth the removing of those things that are shaken, as of things that are made, that those things which cannot be shaken may remain. Wherefore we receiving a kingdom which cannot be moved, let us have grace, whereby we may serve God acceptably with reverence and godly fear: For our God is a consuming fire." (Heb. 12:23-29) All to say that we should serve in reverence without excuse, to the Father through the Lord Jesus Christ.

In Luke 14, we read of the "great supper" where the lord of the house invited many to come, but one after the other had an excuse. Finally the lord said, *"...Go out into the highways and hedges, and compel them to come in, that my house may be filled." (Luke 14:23)* His voice is clear. It is our choice to listen and realize with reverence that the creator of Heaven and earth is talking to you. I want to stand before God one day blameless, having done all I could to bring God's will on earth as it is in Heaven.

"But Christ is something more. He is our SHEPHERD. It is the work of the shepherd to care for the sheep, to feed them and protect them." (D.L. Moody)

Chapter Eleven

Accepting Christ

Someone, somewhere shared the Word of God with you before you finally accepted Jesus Christ as your personal savior. You might have been a stubborn-willed person to keep on turning away the invitation to accept Christ, or the devil might have had you in spiritual bondage nonetheless. The more exposure to the living Word of God, the more the walls of your heart were broken down into wisdom and truth that became undeniably irresistible. *"For the Word of God is quick, and powerful, and sharper than any twoedged sword, piercing even to the dividing asunder of soul and spirit, and of the joints and marrow, and is a discerner of the thoughts and intents of the heart." (Heb. 4:12)*

The Right Path

One knows after accepting Christ the power of the Holy Scriptures, but one needs to realize how personal God's word is in your life and mind. When Hebrews 4:12 states that the Word is a discerner of the thoughts and intents of the heart, this truth continues throughout your whole Christian life. All the thoughts before Salvation had to be divided, cultivated, clarified into right thinking, and made sense enough to make a decision to stand on. You might not understand everything, but after conversion, the Holy Spirit is assuring you that you are on the right path. *"Thy word is a lamp unto my feet, and a light unto my path. I have sworn, and I will perform it, that I will keep thy righteous judgments. I am afflicted very much: quicken me, O Lord, according unto thy word." (Psa. 119:105-107)*

Victory is seen in two ways at this point:

- ❖ The acceptance of Christ as Savior by the Word and the Holy Spirit; *"Behold, I stand at the door, and knock: if any man hear my voice, and open the door, I will come into him, and will sup with him, and he with me." (Rev. 3:20)*

- ❖ A thirst to let the Word change the life of the "New" believer; *"Blessed are they which do hunger and thirst after righteousness: for they shall be filled." (Mat. 5:6)*

Teach the Word

Lives are truly changed by the Bible preached and taught. The problem with the church plan today is limited services with "hit and miss" themes not having a long enough duration. This is not enough saturation on lives and families by the Word of God. It can take years to achieve results in people becoming sold-out believers. The church may have people's undivided attention for a few hours a week, but the enemy has ten times the amount of exposure every single week. On top of all of that, most people don't find a purpose for going to church nor feel comfortable in the setting. Concentration can be the biggest challenge for the hearer as well as the teacher. The most popular poll today, in reality, is that many view the church as being 1. Boring 2. Irrelevant.

The preacher can boldly claim Isaiah 55:11; *"So shall my word be that goeth forward out of my mouth: it shall not return unto me void, but it shall accomplish that which I please, and it shall prosper in the thing whereto I sent it."*

The pleasure belongs to the teacher and the preacher that shares the truth. Accomplishment is a rich return on a job well done.

Step Up and Stand on the Rock

There was once a day when the church and the preaching were more accepted than the time we find ourselves in now. The Bible warns us of such; *"Preach the word; be instant in season, out of season; reprove, rebuke, exhort with all longsuffering and doctrine. For the time will come when they will not endure sound doctrine; but after their own lusts shall they heap to themselves teachers, having itching ears; And they shall turn away their ears from the truth, and shall be turned unto fables. But watch thou in all things, endure afflictions, do the work of an evangelist, make full proof of thy ministry." (II Tim. 4:2-5)*

The supernatural power of God's Word is needed more than ever. Not to say it too lightly, but the fight for the soul has intensified to the point where pure, fire-breathing evangelism is needed everywhere. Accepting Christ is still the victory and the goal, but the fight has become a strategic battle of cutting edge ideas and weapons. A serious ministry for evangelism is needed for winning souls in every Bible-believing, solid-foundational church that is ready to disciple new converts.

The ministerial format of the church has to change to a flow of:

- ❖ Evangelists on the streets and in all social media.
- ❖ The church is to be an inviting place to be with the worship and preaching in balance.
- ❖ The Clergy has the vision to perpetuate the cycle of Salvation to soul-winner (equip the new believer to become a soul-winner).

❖ The discipleship programs and Bible studies are constant (the early church met daily).

Like it or not, the end times are here, and the questions now on everyone's mind are:
- When will Jesus return?
- Who will be in the group of saved going to Heaven?

The Evangelist needs to take his stand and clear position among God and the Pastor to initiate and set in motion full spiritual support for the church to make this all possible.

Prophetic for Today

"Where there is no vision, the people perish..." (Prov. 29:18) The meaning for "vision" was meant by the Hebrews and the 1611 AV to be translated; *"where there is no prophetic vision, the people perish."* Not high idealism, but prophetic leading by Almighty God. Not in man-made plans and strategy, in which all can understand the influence of the enemy using physical and flesh appealing methods; but undoubtedly plans structured by the Holy Spirit and the Lord himself, by much prayer and a vision to lead people to the cross.

Who said the words, *"save yourselves from this untoward generation?"* The clue is that this man preached and three thousand souls were saved and added to the early church. (Acts 2:41)

Peter preached at the time of Pentecost with the power of the Holy Spirit, boldly, unto Jerusalem with the prophetic message of Joel. *"And it shall come to pass in the last days, saith God, I will pour out of my Spirit upon all flesh: and your sons and your daughters shall prophesy, and your young men shall see visions, and your old men shall dream dreams: And on my servants and on my handmaidens I will pour out in those days of my Spirit; and they shall prophesy: And I will shew wonders in heaven above, and signs in the earth beneath; blood, and fire, and vapour of smoke: The sun shall be turned into darkness, and the moon into blood, before that great and notable day of the Lord come: And it shall come to pass, that whosoever shall call on the name of the Lord shall be saved." (Acts 2:17-21)*

The early church had an urgency that we are not experiencing today in our spiritual circles. Peter, no doubt, is reiterating the warning and lament from Joel about the end. It goes from the day of Pentecost, in which we are living in post-Pentecost, where the Holy Spirit will indwell everyone who calls upon him (Rom. 10:13), to the day of the Tribulation where all the judgments will be poured out upon the earth and the unbelieving world. You can't help but notice that Peter doesn't separate these days from the other. All he states is *"...before that great and notable day of the Lord come."* This prophecy was poured out in Peter's day and still continues until the end.

God's Way or Man-Made Religion

One can only wonder if what we are seeing in society today, with all the beautiful buildings and humanitarian efforts from all diverse religious groups, is if the Gospel of Salvation is a priority anywhere in the structure of these ministries. Religious efforts are not the summation of God's intent. To bridge-in the lost has its merits, but somewhere, at some time, the decision for Jesus Christ, of accepting him as Lord and Savior, has to be made.

The excitement of a service to all its degree of inspiration, emotion, assurance, and inherit standing, is still awarded to people getting saved and baptized. Salvation of souls carries the weight of any church service, where the music and heart-tugging moments are needed, but genuine conversion will be enough to keep the people coming back for more. Otherwise, if Salvation is not happening in the church, how many good religious ideas can replace the genuine article? That is the attempt of the majority.

Reformation or Transformation?

"And they continued steadfastly in the apostles' doctrine and fellowship, and in breaking of bread, and in prayers." (Acts 2:42) It takes a body of believers to demonstrate the true commission of the Lord Jesus; in *"doctrine,"* the death, burial, and resurrection is the Gospel of Salvation; in *"fellowship,"* the model of sharing; in *"breaking of bread,"* enjoying the unity; and in *"prayers,"* forging the power of God. The result to the public was awe and wonder because lives were eternally changed. Can a few hours a week at church do this transformation of lives as we practice in our present-day churches?

"Therefore if any man be in Christ, he is a new creature: old things are passed away; behold, all things are become new. And all things are of God, who hath reconciled us to himself by Jesus Christ, and hath given to us the ministry of reconciliation." (II Cor. 5:17-18) Easy believe-ism is a lack of genuine conversion. Salvation can be accepted and a miraculous change will occur, but a large percentage of people that seemingly accept Christ drop out of church or fall back into sinful lifestyles. One can only speculate about their true conversion. Reforming, or joining the group, is

not the same as transforming and joining the Lord and his church by genuine repentance. Don't be fooled by the man-made Christian, where there is no redemption and regeneration. The Spirit is willing and always will be, but the flesh of mankind is weak and continues to put forth a futile effort. *"Be not deceived; God is not mocked: for whatsoever a man soweth, that shall he also reap. For he that soweth to his flesh shall of the flesh reap corruption; but he that soweth to the Spirit shall of the Spirit reap life everlasting." (Gal. 6:7-8)* People get saved through the Word, people get saved through the fellowship and prayers, people get saved and baptized into the family of God when the church's efforts are focused on Salvation.

The supernatural transformation is the most remarkable experience of any person's life. The spiritual rebirth is more powerful and life-changing than anything short of being in Heaven than a human will ever experience. The regeneration of the soul is the work of the Holy Spirit to change the spirit of man into the Spirit of God. *"For what man knoweth the things of a man, save the spirit of man which is in him? even so the things of God knoweth no man, but the Spirit of God. Now we have received, not the spirit of the world, but the spirit which is of God; that we might know the things that are freely given to us of God." (I Cor. 2:11-12)*

Proof of Salvation

No longer shall people wander through life with no certain wisdom or direction. I am convinced that mankind was made for God's pleasure, to serve him and none other. We are locked in at the moment we get saved by the Holy Spirit, "sealed" by the spirit according to Ephesians 4:30. People will live better and serve better once we convince ourselves that Jesus is the way, the only way; the truth, the only truth; and he is the only life regardless of what Satan and the world say. We are citizens of Heaven here on a mission to reap the world's harvest before we take our exodus. Remember, we are written in the Lamb's Book of Life, separated from the world. (Rev. 21:27)

"But, I can imagine someone saying, 'What am I to do? I cannot create life. I certainly cannot save myself.' You certainly cannot; and we do not preach that you can. We tell you that it is utterly impossible to make a man better without Christ; but that is what men are trying to do. They are trying to patch up this 'old-Adam' nature. THERE MUST BE A NEW CREATION. Regeneration is a new creation; and if it is a new creation, it must be the work of God. In the first chapter of Genesis, man does not appear. There is no one there but God. Man is not there to help or take part. When God created the earth, He was alone. When Christ redeemed the world, He was alone." (D.L. Moody)

The most asked question of every believer that is engaged into God's service is, "what is God's Will for my life?" The believer may be serving in the church, and that is mostly the case, and the sense of self-definition comes over them and the question is overwhelming. "How will God use me," or "what is my spiritual gift?" At that point, they are no longer questioning about their eternal security, but the babe in Christ is wanting meat and ready for a taste of something more challenging. A senior Pastor of any church can recognize this new spiritual drive and motivation of some of their young servants… or should we call them young evangelists? The Will of God will find you, is the correct answer for those who are asking. The access to reach out for more service should come in the form of reaching the lost for Jesus Christ. Don't hold back anyone who is ready to serve with a courageous stroke of spiritual tenacity. Jesus sent his disciples out two by two into the field to "get their feet wet," so to say. It's time for consummation with evangelism, not to merely teach them how to be a good Christian. *"For we are labourers together with God: ye are God's husbandry, ye are God's building. According to the grace of God which is given unto me, as a wise masterbuilder, I have laid the foundation, and another buildeth thereon. But let every man take heed how he buildeth thereupon. For other foundation can no man lay than that is laid, which is Jesus Christ." (I Cor. 3:9-11)*

As I have mentioned before, the program of Evangelism has to be a priority in every church if you want to survive and know for sure that you and your church will be supported by God. Why? Because God gave His only begotten Son to come to this world to seek the lost and save them, giving his life for that purpose on a cruel cross. The purpose and the life-blood of the church is evangelizing. The "Great Commission" is to *"Go ye therefore, and teach all nations, baptizing them in the name of the Father, and of the Son, and of the Holy Ghost: Teaching them to observe all things whatsoever I have commanded you: and, lo, I am with you always, even unto the end of the world. Amen." (Mat. 28:19-20)* God's power and presence is enough to stand on and purpose your life with hope, courage, vigor, love, and victory.

Chapter Twelve

Revival Comes by Salvation

It is clear to see in America and all over the world the need for Revival. Does this mean raise the "dead, uninspired Christian?" Or does it mean to bring down fire from above, somewhat like Elijah at Mt. Carmel?

Evil has taken its stand, sin has become commonplace, the human conscience has become seared to the point of desensitization, and the truth seems to fall on deaf ears. The vacuum of this age and era has come to a serious level to usher in a full-blown righteous crusade, Spiritual Awakenings or the most popular term, "Revival."

According to *Christian History Magazine*, there are five elements of spiritual awakenings:

1. Awakenings are usually preceded by a time of spiritual depression, apathy, and gross sin, in which a majority of nominal Christians are hardly different from the members of a secular society, and the churches seem to be asleep.
2. An individual or small group of God's people becomes conscious of their sins and backslidden condition, and vows to forsake all that is displeasing to God.
3. As some Christians begin to yearn for a manifestation of God's power, a leader or leaders arise with prophetic insight into the causes and remedies of the problems, and a new awareness of the Holy and pure character of the Lord is present.

4. The awakenings of Christians occurs: many understand and take part in a higher spiritual life.
5. An awakening may be God's means of preparing and strengthening His people for future challenges or trials. 10

Gypsy Smith, a well- known Evangelist of yesteryear, was asked how to start a revival, and he answered, *"Go home, lock yourself in your room, kneel down in the middle of the floor. Draw a chalk mark all around yourself and ask God to start a revival inside the chalk mark."* What he was alluding to is that revival starts with you and God.

God Calls Leaders with the Word

Leaders throughout the ages have been quick to point out and give lectures and sermons on the climate of society, but rarely do you hear solutions to confront these issues. Jesus said; *"Think not that I am come to send peace on earth: I came not to send peace, but a sword." (Mat. 10:34)* Translated: the conflict can only be dealt with by a swift, powerful sword of the Lord, in which Ephesians 6 calls the "sword of the Spirit," which is the "Word of God" (hrema, word). With the "helmet of salvation" (pelikos, helmet), which is the message of sure protective hope. *"And take the helmet of salvation, and the sword of the Spirit, which is the word of God: Praying always with all prayer and supplication in the Spirit, and watching thereunto with all perseverance and supplication for all saints."(Eph. 6:17-18)* The image of the battle-ready soldier bearing the whole armor of God is portrayed with every piece of equipment in place. Let's look at the three that are most prevalent; the sword, the helmet, and the prayers. A leader has to have the determination to use the Word as a two-edged sword to pierce hearts and souls, where the helmet of Salvation

10 *Christian History Magazine*, "Patterns of Spiritual Renewal" Issue 23, pg. 7

message has to be skillfully placed. Quick and powerful is the Word, but it takes the careful mind of Christ to use the word. Pastors intentionally and prayerfully plan revivals in the church to give the people a full and unapologetic blast of preaching for decisions. Isn't that what society needs, but on a larger scale? Say on a networked scale such as social media. Billy Graham Crusades have been successful for many decades by use of radio and television.

The Present Opportunity

The message of Salvation can flow through the multi-faceted media even at a warp speed today if leaders were determined to build the momentum to a never before seen high level of evangelism. I have people say that they have never heard the Gospel. That is inexcusable for today. Jesus' statement of the "field is white (or ripe) for harvest," has never been more true than the day we are living in when evil is marching globally. The gates of Hell shall not prevail against the church, as we know, but D. James Kennedy called these satanic moves hammers. *"Try as they might, our present-day critics who hammer away at Christ, the church, and the Bible, will not succeed in the long run. The anvil of God will endure forever. The Word has endured through all the ages, and it will endure the present attack on it from all sides."* [11]

The playing field is level, the battle is on, and the Christians know who wins. We can only advance against the enemy if genuine Salvation has been won. Anything else is as the Apostle Paul states; *"I therefore so run, not as uncertainly; so fight I, not as one that beateth the air." (I Cor. 9:26)* The church-world of grandstanding with no

11 D. James Kennedy, "The Gates of Hell Shall Not Prevail", Thomas Nelson Publishers, pg.56

Salvation results is costly, time consuming, and empty at best. I will repeat myself by saying that services that yield souls saved, people walking the aisle to the altar, and constant baptizing, hold all the excitement that God ever intended for churches. The gates of Hell can't stop the church from its mandated commission.

The church cannot leave its first love as the church at Ephesus in Revelation 2, *"Remember therefore from whence thou art fallen, and repent, and do the first works ..."* *(Rev. 2:5)* Return back to solid, decision driven Salvation messages from a fiery pulpit!

The Appointment

"Forasmuch then as we are the offspring of God, we ought not to think that the Godhead is like unto gold, or silver, or stone, graven by art or man's device. And the times of this ignorance God winked at; but now commandeth all men every where to repent: Because he hath appointed a day, in which he will judge the world in righteousness by that man whom he hath ordained; whereof he hath given assurance unto all men, in that he hath raised him from the dead." (Acts 17: 29-31) Only God knows when the fullness of times will come to fruition in his own mind. The days of images and statues are over, and God will not wink at or overlook anymore. The worship of showing God your faith is all taken into consideration, and we surely bless God with our lifted hearts, but the day of faith without works is dead being alone.

According to James chapter 2, we can give to the poor and show our faith with works, *"...I will shew thee my faith by my works."(James 2:18)* In verse 19, to follow that thought, *"Thou believest that there is one God; thou doest well: the devils also believe, and tremble."* Is this helping the poor or unfortunate Christianity? I say to put the devils on the run with the Word of God, not to tremble at our works only, but to fear at our presence!

You are not where you are as the ministers of God, a royal priesthood by accident. God chose you to be in this position. The challenge at hand is to prepare yourself for hard-core evangelism and to watch God move on the churches across our land in Revival because we are moving forward in nourishing, cultivating, and plowing for God to give the increase.

The Will of God is that all should come to repentance. With no repentance, there is no salvation and no Revival. Everything is meant to synchronize to work as a spiritual force to see our culture change for the Kingdom of God.

A Grain of Mustard Seed

"The kingdom of heaven is like to a grain of mustard seed, which a man took, and sowed in his field: Which indeed is the least of all seeds: but when it is grown, it is the greatest among herbs, and becometh a tree, so that the birds of the air come and lodge in the branches thereof." (Mat. 13:31-32) Many are familiar with this passage of scripture and have taught on the subject of the kingdom of Heaven. Each man symbolizes Christ, the field is the world, and the seed, of course, is the word of God that tells of Christ and His kingdom.

Know that Jesus is referring to the Early Church, how the start was very small with a group of apostles meeting in obscure locations teaching of this Jesus that had been put to death on a Roman cross, but rose again from the dead, and was now commissioned to go *"in Jerusalem, and in all Judaea, and in Samaria, and unto the uttermost part of the earth." (Acts 1:8)* They obeyed the Lord and began to spread the Gospel, as difficult and dangerous as it became. The seed has been planted, and with the power of God, the smallest seed began to germinate in the hearts of everyone who heard it, even the enemy.

"For evangelist Bob Cryder, revival in the United States is not a matter of 'if,' but 'when.' I honestly believe that the coming outpouring (of the Holy Spirit) is being prepared in some hidden, unknown, small place. It may be in a city that is unknown and overlooked. As with Jeremiah Lanphier and Evan Roberts, God, I believe , will lay hold of one who, though unknown, is mighty with God in prevailing prayer. This person's unseen faithfulness will catch God's hand and bring His anointing. How deeply I praise God for the large gatherings around revival in our day, but I believe spiritual awakening will come from the 'small and unknown' – that way God will get all the glory." 12 *(Tom Phillips)*

The church today, all around the world, has become the tree that has grown up from that early evangelism. The branches are large, lofty, and spread out world-wide. But as the parable goes, the birds of the air lodge on its branches. Realize the scripture here is talking about the birds being agents of evil as in Revelation 18:2; *"...a cage of every unclean and hateful bird."* (in the fall of Babylon). In Jeremiah 5:27, *"As a cage is full of birds, so are their houses full of deceit..."* The outstanding growth of the church has provided roosting places for the leering view of the enemy to perch upon every lofty place, ready to devour the fruit from the church. Genuine Salvation is the fruit that the agents can't touch, but the aimless fruit from other teachings, that is not sound doctrine, will be devoured.

Revival Comes From Salvation

Remember that Salvation comes first before anything

12 Tom Phillips, "Revival Signs", Vision House Publishing, pg. 234

else can be added to a person's understanding of scripture or spiritual fruit. This has to stay the premise in every denomination or assembly. Directing people in the right direction has to start with the Holy Spirit in the sealing of eternal life; *"In whom ye also trusted, after that ye heard the word of truth, the gospel of your salvation: in whom also after that ye believed, ye were sealed with that holy Spirit of promise." (Eph. 1:13)*

Why do we need revival in the first place? Because Christians have let the influence of the enemy sway them from the truth. *"All of us wish we could stay on the mountain top all the time. Surely Christians may have blessings day by day. God has provided victory for a Christian all the time. There need be no relapses, no periods of defeat, no fruitlessness. There is abundant power for every Christian all the time. Yet the plain, simple fact is that all God's people need reviving frequently. People do not stay on the mountain of transfiguration, they must return to the valley of suffering."* 13 *(John R. Rice)*

But, consider that waves may sweep over the rock, but don't move the rock. Meaning that the Salvation is deep seated by God and will remain no matter what utter nonsense some teachings are resorting to today. (I Tim. 1:4-10) Revival and reawakening are real and needed to revive the soul back to the Lord, and every Minister that has true intentions is to stay on track with the word of truth and recognize that the flock is getting off course and be willing to do something about it. All others have an agenda and purposely lead people adrift.

Revival comes from Salvation; the recharge of the soul is the primary purpose. The evangelism from the soul is the fruit thereof. The evidence of this book brings around to a

13 John R. Rice, "The SOUL-WINNER'S FIRE", Sword of The Lord Publishers, pg.60

complete circle that; ***"The fruit of the righteous is a tree of life; and he that winneth souls is wise." (Prov. 11:30)*** The saved will win the lost; that is their fruit, and when the souls of the Christians are right with God, then the "Great Commission" becomes now "Our Greatest Opportunity." A combined effort among churches today can change the culture by emphasizing and publicizing, "Salvation First," and bring the great "Spiritual Awakening" once again. Amen.

"FOR THE WAGES OF SIN IS DEATH; BUT THE GIFT OF GOD IS ETERNAL LIFE THROUGH JESUS CHRIST OUR LORD." ROMANS 6:23

THE SOUL IS ETERNAL:

I KNOW EVEN AFTER I DIE, MY SOUL WILL GO INTO AN ETERNITY IN HEAVEN OR HELL.

I HAVE SINNED AGAINST GOD AND I NEED HIM TO FORGIVE ME SO I CAN RECEIVE THE GIFT OF ETRNAL LIFE.

CONFESS WITH YOUR MOUTH AND BELIEVE IN YOUR HEART:

I BELIEVE THAT JESUS CAME TO DIE ON THE CROSS FOR MY SINS, SO I ASK GOD AT THIS TIME TO FORGIVE ME OF ALL OF MY SINS, AND I ASK JESUS TO COME INTO MY HEART AND SAVE MY SOUL THAT I MAY SPEND ETERNITY IN HEAVEN.

MY PROMISE:

I WILL LIVE FOR HIM AND TELL OTHERS HOW HE CAME TO EARTH, DIED ON THE CROSS, AND ROSE AGAIN TO SAVE ME.

IN JESUS' NAME. AMEN

BIBLIOGRAPHY

1 Vance Havner, Nelson's Complete Book of Stories, Illustrations,& Quotes, 499

2 www.barna.org, Is Evangelism Going Out of Style?, Dec. 17, 2013

3 John R. Rice, The SOUL-WINNERS FIRE, The Sword of the Lord Publishing, 21,60

4 Charles Stanley, Walking Wisely, Thomas Nelson Publishers, 16

5 Charles Stanley, Confronting Casual Christianity, BROADMAN PRESS,66

6 Tim LaHaye, Jerry B. Jenkins, Are We Living in the End Times, Tyndale House Publishers,7

7 Bill Bright, How To Tell Others About Christ, Worldwide Challenge, April 17, 1993, Robert J. Morgan, Nelson's Complete Book of Stories, Illustrations, & Quotes, 799

8 D. James Kennedy, The Gates of Hell Shall Not Prevail, Thomas Nelson Publishers, 56, 216

9 Rick Warren, The Purpose Driven Life, Zondervan, 281

10 Christian History Magazine, Patterns of Spiritual Renewal, Issue 23, 7

11 D. James Kennedy, "The Gates of Hell Shall Not Prevail", Thomas Nelson Publishers, pg.56

12 Tom Phillips, Revival Signs, Vision Signs, Vision House Publishing, 234

13 John R. Rice, "The SOUL-WINNER'S FIRE", Sword of The Lord Publishers, pg.60